11/03

20.95

I0699469

Historical American Biographies

# J. EDGAR HOOVER

## Powerful FBI Director

Tom Streissguth

**Enslow Publishers, Inc.**

| | |
|---|---|
| 40 Industrial Road | PO Box 38 |
| Box 398 | Aldershot |
| Berkeley Heights, NJ 07922 | Hants GU12 6BP |
| USA | UK |

http://www.enslow.com

**Library of Congress Cataloging-in-Publication Data**

Streissguth, Thomas, 1958–
  J. Edgar Hoover : powerful FBI Director / Tom Streissguth.
     p. cm. — (Historical American biographies)
  Includes bibliographical references and index.
  Summary: Discusses the life and controversy of J. Edgar Hoover, former
  chief of the Federal Bureau of Investigation,
     ISBN 0-7660-1623-4
  1.  Hoover, J. Edgar (John Edgar), 1895–1972—Juvenile literature.
  2.United States. Federal Bureau of Investigation—Juvenile literature.
  3.  Police—United States—Biography—Juvenile literature. 4. Government
  executives—United States—Biography—Juvenile literature. [1. Hoover, J.
  Edgar (John Edgar), 1895–1972. 2. Police. 3. United States. Federal Bureau of
  Investigation—History.] I. Title. II. Series.
     HV7911.H6 S77  2002
     363.25'092—dc21                                              2001003143

Printed in the United States of America

10 9 8 7 6 5 4 3 2 1

**To Our Readers:** We have done our best to make sure all Internet addresses in this book
were active and appropriate when we went to press. However, the author and the publisher
have no control over and assume no liability for the material available on those Internet
sites or on other Web sites they may link to. Any comments or suggestions can be sent by
e-mail to comments@enslow.com or to the address on the back cover.

**Illustration Credits:** © Corel Corporation, p. 13; Enslow Publishers, Inc., p. 16;
Federal Bureau of Investigation, pp. 4, 6, 29, 45, 48, 50, 52; Library of Congress,
pp. 22, 30, 34, 37, 46, 69, 81, 83, 102, 105; National Archives, pp. 61, 113.

**Cover Illustration:** Federal Bureau of Investigation (Background and
Hoover Portrait)

# CONTENTS

*J. Edgar Hoover*

# 1

# "DON'T SHOOT, G-MEN!"

The crime took place in Oklahoma, on July 23, 1933. Kidnappers took Charles Urschel, a wealthy businessman, into their custody. They drove him across miles of quiet, dusty back roads. They locked him into an empty room. Their ransom note demanded $200,000.

A small group of federal investigators began the search. Eight days after the kidnapping, the family of Charles Urschel paid the ransom, and Urschel went free. On the next day, agents of the Bureau of Investigation (later renamed the Federal Bureau of Investigation) spoke with him.

His captors had blindfolded him, Urschel explained, and driven him to a farm. He had tried to

memorize the left and right turns, and to guess the distance he traveled. He was kept in a room, unable to see but able to hear quite well. Twice a day, at the same time every day, he heard an airplane. Whenever Urschel heard the plane pass overhead, he had asked the kidnappers for the time. He also marked the time of a passing storm, and noted the strange taste of the water.

The agents wrote down these clues. They examined plane schedules, weather reports, and highway maps. They also asked questions of the local police. They found out about a woman

*George "Machine Gun" Kelly had already served time in prison before being sought by the Bureau of Investigation for the kidnapping of Charles Urschel.*

named Kathryn Kelly who, they learned from certain witnesses, had been scheming about a kidnapping that summer. They knew Kelly as the wife of George "Machine Gun" Kelly, a notorious local gangster.

Just a few years before, the Urschel case probably would not have been solved. But since the early 1920s, Director J. Edgar Hoover had built the Bureau of Investigation up from a small federal task force into the most modern crime-fighting outfit in the world. He had built a crime laboratory and trained college graduates to become skilled investigators. He had fought for the bureau by making speeches and writing articles, and each year, he had persuaded members of the United States Congress to increase the bureau's appropriation—the amount of money it could spend.

Hoover knew that the time was right for the Bureau of Investigation. A crime wave was spreading across the Midwest. Bank robbers, thieves, and kidnappers were running wild across the Plains. Innocent people were being hurt or killed. Hoover wanted the public to know that the Bureau of Investigation was on the job, fighting crime, supporting local police, and standing up for law-abiding citizens.

On September 26, agents of the Bureau of Investigation tracked down Kathryn Kelly in

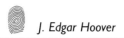 

Memphis, Tennessee. On the same day, they raided a nearby farm—where they found Machine Gun Kelly. When the agents and local police burst into the hideout, Kelly gave up without a fight. He dropped his gun and pronounced his last words as a free man: "Don't shoot, G-Men!"[1]

The next day, Director Hoover told the story to the press. The legend of the G-Man—the "government man"—was born. The unarmed men of his little-known Bureau of Investigation had cracked a sensational crime. There would be many more, but Machine Gun Kelly and the kidnapping of Charles Urschel would put J. Edgar Hoover's bureau in the headlines and on the map for good.

# 2

# SEWARD SQUARE

In the center of Washington, D.C., just a few blocks from the U.S. Capitol Building, lays Seward Square. One hundred years ago, quiet and orderly homes surrounded the square. Many of the people who lived there worked for the government, in one of the many federal buildings scattered across the city. They were clerks, officials, secretaries, and managers. In return for their work and their loyalty, they had a secure job for life and a respectable place in society.

Many of these families remained in government service for several generations. Children—mostly sons—would follow in the footsteps of their fathers. Generation after generation worked for the United

States government and lived within the city limits of Washington, D.C. One such family, the Hoovers, lived at 413 Seward Square.

## The New Hoover

New Year's Day, 1895, brought a special celebration to the Hoover household. That day marked the arrival of the family's youngest child, John Edgar Hoover.

J. E., as his family called him, had one older brother, Dickerson, Jr., and an older sister named Lillian. His mother, Annie Marie Scheitlin Hoover, had also given birth to a daughter in 1890, but this child had died of diphtheria in 1893.

In many ways, Annie Marie Scheitlin Hoover favored John Edgar. She kept a very strict watch over her children. She kept discipline, taught lessons, and brought her family to church every Sunday. Annie's husband, Dickerson Naylor Hoover, worked as chief of the Printing Division of the United States Coast and Geodetic Survey. Dickerson Hoover had a secure, lifelong job in the federal civil service. Dickerson could keep his position as long as he was capable of carrying out his duties.

But despite the security, Dickerson saw himself as a failure. He did not advance or gain new responsibilities, and he often felt frustrated. He sometimes suffered from depression. The depression and frustration grew worse as he grew older, and at times got so bad that he could not work at all.

John Edgar felt much closer to his mother, who doted on him throughout her life. He would live with her, and stay in the house where he grew up, until the day she died.

On one occasion, J. E. did defy his mother's wishes. Although his family was Lutheran, he began attending a Presbyterian church. He had come under the influence of Donald McLeod, a Presbyterian minister.

McLeod held a very strong sense of good and evil, right and wrong. He held up an example of obedience and service to those in his church. J. E. accepted his teachings with enthusiasm. Under McLeod's influence, J. E. began teaching Sunday school and considered, for a time, becoming a minister himself.

At home, J. E. learned to keep a tidy room and a well-ordered house. In 1908, when he was thirteen, he began a diary, in which he kept records of what he did, of the money he made and spent, and of changes in the weather. In an interview, his niece Dorothy remembered that, "All the family had that horrible thing about organization. Everything had to be organized and catalogued, and the pictures had to be straight on the wall—always. It sounds crazy, but we were all like that."[1]

## Doing Well

John Edgar Hoover went to Washington's Central High School, and although he did well in his studies, he struggled with some problems. He was small and spoke with a stutter. He realized at an early age that to overcome such physical problems, he would have to wage a hard battle.

John Edgar joined the debating class at Central High. He practiced his debating every day, sometimes for hours at a time. He taught himself to spot the weak points in the words and logic of his opponents. In debating contests, John Edgar easily derailed his opponents' trains of thought.

John Edgar learned to speak well and study hard. But he admired discipline and patriotism above all. At Central High, he joined the Cadet Corps, a student organization that held military drills on campus. Just as in the real military, they organized their members in ranks. By his senior year, John Edgar was a captain and in command of Company B of the Cadets. On March 4, 1913, he proudly led his company down Pennsylvania Avenue in the inaugural parade for President Woodrow Wilson.

That spring, John Edgar Hoover graduated. Dickerson Hoover was suffering nervous breakdowns, and the Hoover family was still struggling. John Edgar had to decide whether to leave home and attend college, or to stay and support his family. He chose to stay.

## Study, Work, and Information

Hoover enrolled in night classes at George Washington University, where he began the study of law. At the same time, he took a job at the Library of Congress, the immense federal library that holds nearly every work published in the United States. He began as a messenger at a salary of thirty dollars a month and soon became a cataloger.

Hoover learned almost as much at the Library of Congress as he did at George Washington

*While working at the Library of Congress, Hoover first drew on his talent for organizing and collecting information.*

University. The library stacks held millions of books, magazines, and government documents. The librarians and clerks used a complex numbering system to keep track of each separate work under their control. To find a specific book, a visitor had to search through a huge catalogue of small index cards.

Hoover soon learned the Library of Congress classification system by heart. He knew where every kind of book could be found. He also knew what number to assign to new books that arrived. He carried around in his head the layout of the entire Library, a maze of card catalogues, hallways, offices, and shelves. He held almost as much information in his head as the catalogue carried on its millions of small index cards.

Hoover had a talent for information—how to find it, collect it, and organize it. But a career at the Library of Congress did not interest him. In 1916, he received his bachelor of law degree from George Washington University Law School. In the next year, he earned a master's degree and took a job as a clerk at the United States Department of Justice.

# 3

# THE
# DEPARTMENT
# OF JUSTICE

While Hoover was attending night school, a war was being fought in Europe. Rival alliances among the nations of Europe had sparked an arms race and a fight over territory and resources. Now the armies of Germany and Austria were battling France, Great Britain, and Russia. Although the United States did not join the war when it started in 1914, Congress had passed a law to draft young men into the military.

As the battles raged in Europe, the United States was slowly but surely drawn into the conflict. On April 2, 1917, President Woodrow Wilson asked Congress for a declaration of war on Germany. Four

*J. Edgar Hoover lived, was schooled, and worked in Washington, D.C., for almost his entire life. Washington, D.C., borders the Potomac River and is sandwiched between the states of Maryland and Virginia.*

days later, Congress voted in favor, and the United States officially entered World War I.

Many members of the Justice Department volunteered for the army. But John Edgar Hoover had reached an important point in his life: the start of his professional career. Although he had been a proud and dedicated member of the Central High

**Rounding Up the Enemy**

When the United States entered World War I in 1917, the attorney general and the Department of Justice suddenly had a very big job to handle. By a proclamation signed by President Woodrow Wilson on April 6, all aliens resident in the United States who came from a hostile country, such as Germany, could be arrested for owning guns or explosives, possessing coded messages or radio transmitters, or approaching closer than one-half mile to any military installation, arms manufacturing plant, or port. They could not leave the country, and they were barred from declaring in public or writing anything that could be considered an attack on the federal government or the U.S. Congress.

With these restrictions, the Justice Department arrested more than four thousand aliens during the war. But the wartime campaign proved to be just a starting point for the sweeping roundups of suspected radicals and Reds that were to come, and in which J. Edgar Hoover would play an important role within the Bureau of Investigation.

Cadets, he had no interest in joining the army, putting his future on hold, and leaving his mother behind to fend for herself.

That same spring, Dickerson Hoover suffered another nervous breakdown. The United States Coast and Geodetic Survey forced him to resign from his position. He had no pension (a regular payment after retirement), and he was too old to start a new career. Dickerson and Annie Hoover had to depend on their sons for support.

## Rising in the Ranks

John Edgar Hoover was up to the task. He was a hard worker who stayed at the Justice Department late and who showed up for more work on the weekends. Promotions came easily, as many members of the department now wore Army uniforms and lived in Europe.

As he rose within the ranks of the department, Hoover gained new responsibility. He won a promotion to assistant to John Lord O'Brian, a special assistant to the attorney general (the attorney general himself served as the head of the Justice Department). Hoover also became head of the Enemy Alien Registration Section.

In this position, Hoover's job was to collect and organize information on spies, radicals, and draft-dodgers. During World War I, the United States passed strict laws against espionage (spying) as well as sedition (speaking or writing to promote disorder and undermine the government). Those suspected of opposing the war effort were arrested and, in some cases, forced to leave the country. Especially suspect were foreigners, such as Germans. Russians also came under suspicion, because their country was going through a Communist revolution.

In the fall of 1917, the communists (or "Bolsheviks") had overthrown the Russian government. Russia became a Communist nation, in which the state owned all property, all homes, all businesses, all factories, and all the means of production. Only one party remained legal—the Communist party. Communism's leaders believed that their system represented the world's future, and that each country would eventually establish its own Communist government.

The most famous Russians in the United States were Emma Goldman and Alexander Berkman. Both were communists (also known as "Reds," after the color of Russian Communist flags), and both were suspected of spying on the United States. John Edgar Hoover looked on Goldman and Berkman, and others who thought like them, as a great danger to the country's security. He felt certain that these Bolsheviks were planning to overthrow the federal government. He helped the government prosecute

the pair in a federal court and, after they were found guilty, arranged for them to be deported (sent out of the country). Along with 247 other anarchists, communists, and foreign radicals, Berkman and Goldman were put on board the *Buford*, an Army transport that sailed from New York to St. Petersburg, Russia, in December 1919.

Hoover's talent for collecting information served him well in these tasks. To find suspects, he collected information from many different sources. The department paid informers to supply the names of socialists, communists, and radicals. Brochures and articles written by suspects were collected into thick files. Hoover also received information from workers who spied on their coworkers. Ordinary police officers, who saw and heard many things on city streets, passed on what they knew. The informers believed they were working for a good cause: to help the United States win the war in Europe.

Every scrap of information Hoover received found its way into a file. Each file carried a number, which could be found by looking through a long, alphabetical index. It was similar to the catalogue system Hoover had learned at the Library of Congress. Hoover adapted this system to manage a mountain of information on suspected radicals, saboteurs, spies, and communists—especially communists. Anyone suspected of espionage, sabotage, or sedition against the United States government made it onto his lists and his indexes. He supplied the information whenever the Justice Department sought to jail or deport such undesirables from the country.

## The Master of Secrets

The war ended in November 1918. But a war at home continued. A wave of bombings took place in June 1919. The bombs were sent to the homes of business leaders, judges, and politicians. One of the bombs exploded on the doorstep of Attorney General A. Mitchell Palmer. The bomber had accidentally dropped the explosive device, blowing himself to bits.

Frightened by his brush with death, Palmer ordered an investigation. He suspected communists and foreign-born radicals of carrying out the attack. He wanted these people rounded up and deported.

Congress agreed to spend $2 million for this effort. With this money, Palmer set up the General Intelligence Division (GID) of the Justice Department. The GID officially opened for business on August 1, 1919.

Palmer named John Edgar Hoover as the first director of the GID. Hoover's job was to gather and coordinate all information on suspects, no matter what the source of that information. The GID

collected names, addresses, writings, speeches, photographs, news reports, mail, and many other kinds of data. The information came from a variety of sources: newspapers, brochures, private detective agencies, private companies, police departments, and captured mailing lists, which organizations such as the Communist party used to communicate with their members. The agents of the GID also watched meetings and demonstrations and used information gathered during the many industrial strikes that were occurring at that time.

Hoover set up another index card system to organize the GID files. The cards were numbered and cross-indexed. This allowed Hoover and his aides to look up personal information on nearly five

hundred thousand individuals. Hoover became the master of secrets, a collector who could not buy, steal, or borrow enough of what was most precious to him:

*Attorney General A. Mitchell Palmer (pictured) respected Hoover's skills and named him first director of the General Intelligence Division of the Justice Department in 1919.*

information. He learned and remembered more about leftists (those wanting to reform or overthrow the presiding government) and radicals than anybody else in the government.

The Justice Department had many weapons that helped Hoover in this fight. One of the most important of these was a small detective force that had been established by Attorney General Joseph Bonaparte in 1908. At first, this group had no name. In the next year it would be called the Bureau of Investigation.

The Bureau of Investigation looked into federal crimes, which included embezzlement (illegally using someone else's property for one's own use), fraud (illegally misrepresenting the truth in order to gain something of value from someone), and other "white-collar" crimes. Bureau agents also investigated cases of prostitution and the illegal shipment of goods across state lines.

In the search for radicals and Reds, the bureau proved very useful to John Edgar Hoover.

## The Palmer Raids

Meanwhile, the Justice Department, under the direction of Attorney General A. Mitchell Palmer, prepared for a great, sweeping roundup of suspected radicals. A nationwide raid took place on January 2, 1920. Agents and local police arrested more than three thousand people. The agents used blank warrants—documents that gave them the authority to arrest people for no particular reason. They took the suspects down to jail, then filled out the warrants with a cause for the arrest.

The arrest reports were all sent to Hoover. The suspects were kept in jail for a few weeks, then put on trial for spying, sedition, conspiracy, and other crimes. Those found guilty, and who were not U.S. citizens, could be deported.

But inside the government, not everybody went along with the Palmer Raids, as these arrests were called. One opponent was Louis Post, the acting secretary of labor. By law, the Department of Labor had the power to deport noncitizens living in the United States. Not only did Post have the authority to deport people, but he also had the authority to allow them to remain. He looked on the Palmer Raids as an abuse of power by the Justice Department. Eventually, he blocked most of the deportations.

In the meantime, Palmer and the GID warned of an impending revolution on May Day (May 1). The public was not yet convinced, however. When the U.S. Congress held hearings on the Palmer Raids, Hoover accompanied Palmer to the U.S. Capitol to advise him during his testimony. Palmer and Hoover strongly defended the raids and warned of the threat the United States was still facing from radicals and communists.

But when May Day came and went without the revolution Palmer had warned of, the public lost interest and Palmer quickly lost support. Newspapers ridiculed the attorney general's dire predictions of revolution. Palmer had planned to run for president in 1920, but after the peaceful May Day of that year, he saw his political career come to an abrupt end.

Hoover and the GID held onto their files and maintained their network of informants in labor and radical organizations. Hoover opened secret files on all those who had opposed the Palmer Raids and made up a confidential list of enemies. He spotted the nation's enemies in many places, yet still saw himself as a defender of freedom and constitutional rights. In 1924, while talking to Roger Baldwin, the founder of the American Civil Liberties Union (ACLU), he claimed that, "If I can leave my desk each day with the knowledge that I have in no way violated any of the rights of the citizens of this country . . . then I shall feel satisfied."[1]

# 4

# THE HARDING YEARS

In 1920, Warren G. Harding, a member of the Republican party, was elected as the 29th president of the United States. Harding was inaugurated in early 1921. A new administration had arrived in Washington.

Like all presidents, Harding had the right to appoint officials to head important government departments. For the Department of Justice, he appointed Harry Daugherty as the new attorney general. Daugherty had no special qualifications for the job, but he had run Harding's presidential campaign in 1920 and had done more than anyone to help Harding win. For Daugherty, the appointment as attorney general represented a reward for work well done.

John Edgar Hoover did not declare his loyalty to any particular party, nor did he work for any political campaigns. As a resident of Washington, D.C., he did not have a representative in Congress. Like all D.C. residents of that time, he could not even vote. For Hoover, his first loyalty lay with the Department of Justice, his superiors, and his job within the department.

Like his father and most other federal civil servants, Hoover had no interest in running for office. He intended to stay right where he was, whether the president was a democrat or a republican. To keep his job under the new attorney general, Hoover made himself as useful as possible. He offered to show Daugherty secret files on those who opposed Harding, Daugherty, and the new administration. Hoover also sent Daugherty regular memos on the activities of suspected radicals. Hoover's tactics not only protected his job but also earned him a big promotion. Soon after appointing William J. Burns as head of the Bureau of Investigation, Daugherty named Hoover as the assistant chief. The General Intelligence Division was made a part of the Bureau of Investigation.

Hoover still controlled all the files collected by the GID during the war and during the Palmer

Raids. He also controlled a growing network of informants all over the country. He was a hard worker and had a knack for making powerful allies in the government. He no longer had any interest in a career as a lawyer, a minister, or a librarian. He was a government man and he would remain one for life. He would be an investigator—a man who knew secrets and brought his country's and his own enemies to justice.

## Troubles for President Harding

John Edgar Hoover was always very careful to protect his name and his good reputation. He saw himself as a law-abiding, upstanding citizen—a leader and protector of the national community. For this reason, he even changed his name in the early 1920s. At this time, another Washington, D.C. resident with the name of John Edgar Hoover was in trouble for writing bad checks and not paying his bills. When he found out, John Edgar Hoover of the Department of Justice became "J. Edgar Hoover." For the rest of his life, everyone knew the famous national law enforcer as J. Edgar Hoover.[1]

Hoover had the full support of Burns and Daugherty, who admired his hard work and loyalty. Nevertheless, there was trouble at the Justice Department. It all started as the department, and police departments all over the country, faced the biggest law enforcement challenge of history: Prohibition.

The Eighteenth Amendment to the Constitution, which went into effect in January 1920, had prohibited the sale and transport of liquor. But instead of ending the consumption of alcohol, Prohibition brought a new era of lawlessness to the United States. Thousands of "bootleggers," most of them working in the big cities of the East and Midwest, made and sold illegal liquor all over the country. They supplied people willing to pay high prices for their product. A lot of money was at stake, and to protect their business, the bootleggers paid large bribes to police and federal Prohibition agents.

Within the Justice Department, many officials used the Prohibition laws to make money. They took bribes to look the other way when bootleggers were caught.

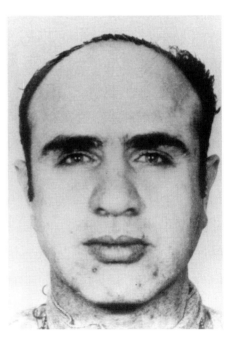

*During Prohibition, criminals like Al Capone profited from the illegal sale of liquor. Capone was eventually jailed for tax evasion.*

They dropped federal cases and protected certain criminals from prosecution. Department officials also accepted money to issue "B" permits. These permits allowed the making of alcohol for legal, medicinal purposes (which then could be turned into illegal liquor).

The Bureau of Investigation (BI) became an important part of the corruption and illegal goings-on. The bureau was used to help the friends, and hinder the enemies, of the Harding administration. Bureau agents opened mail and listened in on telephone conversations. They gathered information on the private lives of thousands of public figures:

*During Prohibition, government agents often raided establishments that illegally sold or manufactured liquor.*

politicians, newspaper editors, even movie and sports stars. Communists and radicals were not the only targets. Anyone who criticized Harding, Daugherty, or the administration could make it into the files of the BI.

At the center of all this activity was J. Edgar Hoover, who was managing the BI. Hoover ordered agents all over the country to gather information on the administration's enemies. He added the information to the files of the BI and provided it to federal prosecutors. Hoover used this information whenever necessary to help his bosses and his friends.

Meanwhile, President Harding and Harry Daugherty found themselves caught up in scandal. Through newspaper reports, the public learned of the Prohibition dealings of the Justice Department. The public also heard rumors that Harding officials had allowed certain oil companies to drill for oil on federal lands in return for bribes. In the spring of 1923, the scandals began to overwhelm President Harding. On August 2, he died of a stroke in a San Francisco hotel. His vice president, Calvin Coolidge, was sworn in as the 30th president.

## Harlan Fiske Stone

President Coolidge had his own reputation to protect. He did not want the Harding scandals to taint his presidency. Early in 1924, he ordered Harry

## Not Fighting Communism

The Palmer Raids of 1920 had turned into a witch hunt, and Attorney General A. Mitchell Palmer had lost all support among the public and the U.S. Congress. Many people were calling for the Bureau of Investigation to be completely abolished. In reaction, the new attorney general, Harlan Fisk Stone ordered J. Edgar Hoover, his new Bureau of Investigation director, to stick to criminal investigations. For the rest of the 1920s, while Hoover was reorganizing the bureau, Communism was the last problem any FBI agent was supposed to think about. The bureau was limited to criminal investigations only. J. Edgar Hoover concerned himself only with reorganizing the bureau and making it the most efficient and progressive agency of the federal government. In 1925, Hoover remarked, "Our bureau carries on no investigations of matters that are not contrary to federal statutes [laws]. There is no federal statute against entertaining radical ideas, and we are wasting no time collecting information that we cannot use."[2]

That policy began to change in 1936, the year President Franklin Roosevelt allowed the FBI to resume domestic surveillance on all suspected opponents of the U.S. government, including suspected Communists.

Daugherty to resign. Coolidge named Harlan Fiske Stone as the new attorney general.

Stone had to decide whether to keep or to fire leaders of the Justice Department. Within the Bureau of Investigation, he fired William J. Burns, but he asked J. Edgar Hoover to stay on as acting director. Hoover had convinced Stone that he was determined to run an honest and scandal-free organization. When the two men met, Stone agreed to Hoover's conditions that: "The Bureau must be divorced from politics and not be a catch-all for political hacks. Appointments must be based on merit. Second, promotions will be made on proved ability and the Bureau will be responsible only to the Attorney General."[3]

Stone let Hoover know that the appointment was temporary. He wanted an end to the corruption and a clean sweep at the BI. Otherwise, he hinted, Hoover could start looking for a new job.

Hoover agreed and went to work, turning the Bureau of Investigation into a strictly run and well-ordered agency. Special agents in charge of local BI offices began reporting to the acting director. Hoover set up a system of merits and demerits to reward BI agents for their efficiency and effectiveness. A strict dress code was put in place. Hoover absolutely forbade any agent to drink alcohol, either

*Even at a young age, director J. Edgar Hoover worked hard to improve the efficiency of the then-called Bureau of Investigation.*

on the job or in private. He laid down the law in one memo that stated,

> I am determined to summarily dismiss from this Bureau any employee whom I find indulging in the use of intoxicants to any degree or extent upon any occasion . . . I, myself, am refraining from the use of intoxicants . . . And I am not, therefore, expecting any more of the field employees than of myself.[4]

Agents were expected to devote their lives to the bureau. Most began working six days a week. They earned letters of praise for success, and letters of censure for failures. Promotions were based on performance, not on seniority or connections. From time to time, the agents had to travel to Washington for training. Bureau officials, and sometimes Hoover himself, arrived at their field offices for surprise inspections.

Hoover set up a single filing system for the entire organization. He also ordered that all evidence collected by BI agents was to be put down on a single, standard form. The BI then turned these forms over to federal prosecutors, who used the information to decide whether or not to bring a case against a suspected criminal. Although BI agents could not make arrests nor carry guns, they helped prosecutors convict a high percentage of the suspects brought to trial.

At home, Hoover ordered his personal life as strictly as he ran the BI. His day ran like clockwork, and he held himself to routines of eating, dressing, traveling, and working that would endure for the rest of his life. Fussy about cleanliness and order, he wanted everything around him kept a certain way—the furniture placed just so, pictures hung on the walls at a certain height, and no books or magazines scattered about. His father had died in 1921, and the house at Seward Square had become a retreat from the world outside, a place where he found nearly all the companionship he needed in the company of his widowed mother.

In the meantime, the reform of the Bureau of Investigation drew notice in the press and among the public. Hoover began to see his name mentioned in the newspapers. Reporters wrote well of him, even though he had come up under the Harding administration. The new Bureau of Investigation even impressed Harlan Fiske Stone. On December 10, 1924, Stone ended Hoover's temporary status. J. Edgar Hoover was now the permanent director of the Bureau of Investigation.

## The Lindbergh Case

In May 1927, Charles Lindbergh became a national hero and the most famous man in the world. Lindbergh had done the impossible: he had flown alone and nonstop across the Atlantic Ocean, in a single-engine plane, the *Spirit of St. Louis*. When he landed at an airfield near Paris, a great crowd of people surrounded him and raised him to their shoulders. Upon his return to the United States, New York City gave Lindbergh the longest ticker-tape parade in the city's history.

To the people of the United States, Lindbergh became an important symbol of courage, skill, and know-how. But on March 1, 1932, Lindbergh became a symbol of something else. He became a victim of the crime and violence that was sweeping the country during the Great Depression. On that

*Before the kidnapping of his son, Charles Lindbergh (right) was very well-known due to his flight in the* Spirit of St. Louis. *The Lindbergh baby kidnapping proved the first major challenge to Hoover as director of the BI.*

night, Lindbergh's infant son, Charles Lindbergh, Jr., was kidnapped from the family's home in Hopewell, New Jersey.

At that time, most states had their own laws against kidnapping. Since there was no single federal law against such an act, most people believed the Bureau of Investigation, a federal agency, would have nothing to do with the case. But most people did not see the world through the eyes of J. Edgar Hoover.

Hoover knew that solving this case would bring valuable publicity to his agency. He ordered that a special BI squad work with the New Jersey state police. The BI would track down every lead it could find, follow up on messages and telephone calls that offered tips on the crime, and describe its progress to the newspapers. Hoover even traveled to New Jersey to meet with Lindbergh personally and offer his assistance.

## Cracking the Case

On April 2, Charles Lindbergh and John F. Condon, a schoolteacher who had volunteered to help Lindbergh, delivered a ransom of fifty thousand dollars to a man in St. Raymond's Cemetery in the Bronx, New York. The United States Treasury Department had included gold certificates with the ransom money. The certificates looked like currency, but they also carried serial numbers that were easy to trace. If the money turned up at a store or bank, the marked bills might help police find the kidnappers.

The man who took the ransom money told Condon and Lindbergh the name of a ship where the baby could be found. But he was lying. Charles Augustus Lindbergh, Jr., was discovered on May 12 near the Lindbergh home in Hopewell. The baby was dead.

Until this time, the Lindbergh case had belonged, officially, to the New Jersey state police. After the discovery of the baby's body, President Herbert Hoover ordered federal agencies to get involved in the case. On June 22, Congress passed a law that made kidnapping a federal crime if the victim was transported across state lines. This "Lindbergh Law" was the first of several new laws that would make the Bureau of Investigation the country's largest and most powerful law-enforcement agency.

As Hoover knew, there was only one problem with the Lindbergh Law. It had still done nothing to catch the kidnappers of Charles Lindbergh's baby. Hoover knew that the reputation and the future of his bureau rested on solving this case.

# 5

# PUBLIC ENEMIES

The Depression that began with the stock market crash of 1929 lasted well into the 1930s. President Herbert Hoover lost by a landslide to democrat Franklin Delano Roosevelt in 1932. The new president decided to appoint Senator Thomas J. Walsh as his attorney general. Walsh was best known among the public for his investigation into the Harding scandals. After his appointment, he announced important changes to come at the Department of Justice, including his intention to fire Hoover. J. Edgar Hoover realized his career at the Bureau of Investigation would soon be coming to an end.

But on March 3, 1933, Walsh died of a heart attack. In his place, Roosevelt appointed Homer S.

Cummings. Hoover immediately made himself as useful as he could to Cummings. Special agents wrote letters to Cummings and Roosevelt, asking that Hoover be kept on as director. Harlan Fiske Stone, who was now a justice on the Supreme Court, also came out in support of Hoover. Impressed by this show of support, Cummings decided on July 30, 1933, to keep Hoover on as director.

## Solving the Lindbergh Case

In September 1934, investigators got a break in the Lindbergh kidnapping case. At a gas station in New York City, a man had used a gold certificate to make his purchase. The attendant at the gas station had noted the serial number of the certificate and the license plate of the car. A search of license records was done. The plate belonged to a Dodge owned by a German immigrant, a carpenter named Bruno Richard Hauptmann.

Soon afterward, police arrested Hauptmann. Although they searched his house, they could find no more ransom money. Deciding to try something else, they had Hauptmann transcribe by hand some newspaper articles which were then sent to Washington. As part of J. Edgar Hoover's efforts to make the bureau as modern as possible and to adopt all the latest scientific crime-fighting methods, Agent Charles Appel had started the famous Bureau

of Investigation crime laboratory in 1932. The handwriting samples were analyzed there.

After lab technicians made a careful check, Appel announced that Hauptmann's handwriting sample matched the handwriting on the Lindbergh ransom note. To make sure of the case, BI agents again searched Hauptmann's house and garage, where they found a hidden stash of gold certificates that matched those passed by John Condon as ransom money.

**The Fingerprint Collector**

J. Edgar Hoover wanted to make the FBI into a scientific crime-fighting agency. He believed the foundation of the new Bureau would be the ordinary fingerprint—a unique record of identity that can never be erased or falsified, and that is different for every individual.

Hoover's ambition was to fingerprint every citizen, whether or not they were criminals, and to keep these fingerprints on file for use by the FBI. Although the FBI never achieved that goal, it did become the nation's main storage warehouse for fingerprints. The bureau gathered copies of every print taken by every police department, the fingerprints of all prisoners and federal employees, and of all members of the military. By the time of J. Edgar Hoover's death, the Bureau had collected about 160 million fingerprints.

But there were problems with the Hauptmann case. At first, John Condon could not identify Hauptmann as the man he had passed the ransom money to. Later, Condon changed his mind. Also, Hauptmann's fingerprints did not match the fingerprints found on the gold certificates. The prosecutor had very little evidence to prove that Hauptmann was the man who had broken into the Lindberghs' house and kidnapped the Lindbergh baby.

Eventually, Bruno Hauptmann was put on trial, and a jury did convict him of the murder of Charles Lindbergh, Jr. He would be executed on April 3, 1936. Hauptmann was one of the first suspects to be convicted on scientific evidence such as handwriting and fingerprints. To the public, much of the credit for solving the case lay with J. Edgar Hoover and the Bureau of Investigation.

## A Shoot-out in Kansas City

The Lindbergh kidnapping was just one of many serious crimes carried out in the wake of the failed Prohibition experiment. Prohibition was responsible for bribery and other forms of corruption in police departments, courtrooms, city halls, and legislatures across the country. Even Prohibition's biggest sup-porters recognized that Americans would drink liquor, legally or illegally, and that no law would change their minds.

The Eighteenth Amendment was repealed in 1933. At this time, the Depression was in full swing. The economy was weak, unemployment was high, and many people suffered poverty, hunger, and desperation. In the Midwest, criminal gangs still roamed the countryside, robbing stores and banks and evading the local police. Their deeds often made headlines across the country. At the same time, J. Edgar Hoover saw to it that the BI made it to page one as often as possible.

The crime that brought the BI into the thick of the national war on crime took place in Kansas City on June 17, 1933. On that day, four BI agents and three local policemen were bringing Frank Nash, a convicted bank robber, through the city's train station. Nash was on his way to the federal prison in Leavenworth, Kansas.

As the group reached their cars on the street outside the station, three men standing nearby suddenly opened fire. Bullets whistled through the air as the agents ducked for cover or fell to the ground. When the gunfire stopped, one BI agent, three policemen, and Frank Nash himself lay dead.

The daring daylight shoot-out, and the attack on agents of the Bureau of Investigation, inspired J. Edgar Hoover to declare a nationwide war on crime. To fight that war, he wanted more authority and more power for the BI. With the support of

Attorney General Cummings, he succeeded. In the next year, Congress passed several new and important laws. It became a federal crime to rob a bank, to transport any kind of stolen property, to assault a government agent, or to attempt to escape the police by crossing state lines. In addition, BI agents were allowed to carry guns, make searches of people and property, and arrest criminal suspects.

Instead of merely conducting investigations, the BI was now acting as a kind of national police force. But it handled only the most serious cases—violations

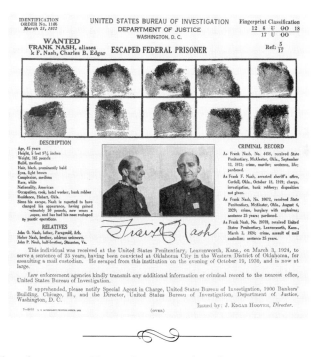

*When the events in Kansas City occurred, authorities were escorting Frank Nash back to the United States Penitentiary in Leavenworth, Kansas. He had escaped from the prison on October 19, 1930.*

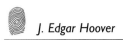
of the sweeping new federal crime laws. It had the authority to arrest bank robbers, kidnappers, and gangsters of all kinds, and chase them all over the country, if necessary.

To back up the new laws, Congress also granted the BI a higher appropriation. With his much improved budget, Hoover updated the BI crime laboratory and hired thousands of new agents. For Hoover, the annual appropriation for the Bureau became an important measure of his personal standing and reputation.

## The Search for John Dillinger

J. Edgar Hoover knew that he was much more than the "nation's top cop"—a nickname the press was

now giving him. He considered the job of swaying public opinion in support of the bureau another very important part of his job. One way to improve the opinion of the public

*Having eluded the Bureau of Investigation numerous times, bank robber John Dillinger quickly became one of the most sought-after criminals in the history of the United States.*

and of Congress was by making sure that the BI arrested its share of famous and dangerous criminals.

In the spring of 1934, the most famous criminal in the country was John Dillinger. A daring bank robber, Dillinger had escaped from the Crown Point, Indiana, jail on March 3. He used a stolen car to cross state lines—making this a case for the BI.

The BI set several traps to catch Dillinger and his gang, but the wily criminal evaded them all. Then, in late April, an anonymous tip reached BI agent Melvin Purvis, head of the BI's Chicago office. The tipster reported that Dillinger was hiding out at a northern Wisconsin resort known as Little Bohemia. Hoover ordered BI agents from St. Paul and Chicago to move in, surround the resort, and arrest Dillinger. He also called newspaper reporters to hint that the bureau was about to capture the nation's most dangerous criminal.

But the raid did not go as planned. As the agents surrounded Dillinger's hideout, a dog began barking, alerting the criminals. When three men ran out of the building and hurried into a waiting car, the agents opened fire and accidentally killed an innocent bystander. In the confusion and gunfire, Dillinger and his gang slipped away. Later, "Baby Face" Nelson, a member of the Dillinger gang, shot it out with several agents and police on a nearby

*Baby Face Nelson, whose real name was Lester M. Gillis, was the ruthless member of Dillinger's gang who gunned down bureau agent Carter Baum in 1934. Nelson had escaped from the State Penitentiary in Joliet, Illinois, two years earlier.*

back road. Nelson escaped after killing agent Carter Baum.

Hoover took Purvis off the case, and put another agent named Sam Cowley in charge of the Dillinger manhunt. He offered a reward of ten thousand dollars to any person responsible for catching Dillinger—dead or alive. To newspaper reporters, he announced that John Dillinger was now "Public Enemy Number One" and the BI's top priority.

## The Woman in Red

Although Purvis was off the case, he still had his job. On July 21, 1934, Indiana police sergeant Martin Zarkovich contacted Purvis with some very interesting information on John Dillinger. An immigrant named Anna Sage (whose real name was Ana Cumpanas) had made an offer. She knew John Dillinger and would help the lawmen arrest him. In exchange, she wanted the reward money.

Purvis relayed the offer to Hoover, who accepted Anna Sage's deal. Sage then told Hoover that she, Dillinger, and another woman were planning to go to a movie the next night. This would be the bureau's best chance yet to nab the slippery Dillinger.

Purvis drew up a plan. He placed himself and several other agents in position outside Chicago's Biograph Theater. Just before the film *Manhattan Melodrama* was scheduled to begin, Anna Sage appeared in a bright orange skirt, which looked red under the theater lights (from this night on, the press and the public would know her, mistakenly, as the "Woman in Red"). The skirt was part of the plan to identify her to the agents.

By telephone, Sam Cowley relayed the information to Hoover, who ordered Purvis not to arrest Dillinger yet. A shoot-out in a crowded movie theater was too risky, so Purvis was to wait outside the theater for Dillinger to appear. While Dillinger

*Anna Sage lured John Dillinger into Chicago's Biograph Theater to see the film* Manhattan Melodrama, *starring Clark Gable, while federal agents waited outside.*

sat inside enjoying the movie, Cowley and several other agents appeared on the scene. Purvis stationed himself near the box office and waited.

Dillinger appeared at the theater door at 10:30 P.M., as the movie was letting out. He sensed immediately that something was wrong. Seeing the plainclothes agents move toward him, he began to run. Purvis followed him up an alley, and ordered Dillinger to stop. Dillinger pulled a gun from his pocket and began firing. Three BI agents instantly returned fire. Purvis did not draw his gun. He did not need to. Public Enemy Number One had gone down in a hail of bullets from the other agents.

Although several bystanders were present, nobody else was hurt. The agents survived the shoot-out without a scratch. Purvis immediately called J. Edgar Hoover and gave him the good news. Hoover then made the announcement to the press. The death of John Dillinger, he knew, would go down as one of the greatest victories in the history of the BI.

## The Trouble with Melvin Purvis

The John Dillinger case made Melvin Purvis famous all over the country, nearly as famous as J. Edgar Hoover himself. Purvis was short, slight, and boyish, but he was also a smart and skilled investigator. Later that year, he won more headlines with the

**Putting Public Enemy No. I on Display**

J. Edgar Hoover always considered the killing of John Dillinger to be one of the highest achievements of his time as FBI director. Soon after Dillinger's death, a plaster cast was made of his face. This "death mask" was one of Hoover's most prized possessions, and one copy of the mask sold at auction in 1991 for ten thousand dollars. The mask can be seen at the FBI museum, along with Dillinger's arsenal of weapons, bulletproof vest, and straw hat.

capture and killing of Charles Arthur "Pretty Boy" Floyd on an Ohio farm. In November, after Sam Cowley was killed in a shoot-out with Baby Face Nelson, Purvis went to the newspapers and declared that he would personally seek revenge for Cowley's death.

However, the fame of Melvin Purvis did not sit well with the BI director. J. Edgar Hoover enjoyed seeing his own name in the papers, and he did not like sharing the spotlight with anyone. For J. Edgar Hoover, no single agent could be more important

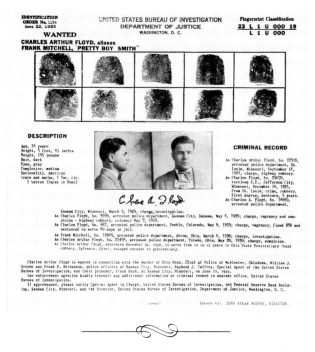

*Melvin Purvis became even more famous when he helped capture and kill "Pretty Boy" Floyd (pictured). Floyd was wanted for the murders of Frank Nash and authorities escorting Nash.*

than the bureau, and no agent could be allowed to challenge the director's position, his authority, or his national fame. He knew Purvis was too popular to be fired, so instead he made Purvis's life as miserable as possible. He sent him to small BI offices on useless inspection tours, and made sure Purvis was assigned only to unimportant cases. In July 1935, Purvis finally resigned from the bureau.

In that same year, the bureau was officially renamed the Federal Bureau of Investigation (FBI). The name reflected the growing power and influence of the bureau, which had become a national investigative agency—the largest and most authoritative in the country. For the next forty years, Hoover would identify himself completely with the FBI, and would try—mostly with success— to shape its agents in his own image. Its successes would be his, and he would take any failures and any public criticism of the bureau very personally. Hoover would have no other job, nor would he resign, nor would he ever be fired, even though a long series of attorneys general had the authority to fire him. Hoover wanted his agents to be "married to the bureau," a claim he could well have made himself until the day he died.

6

# THE WAR AND THE FBI

On December 7, 1941, a huge force of Japanese bombers, torpedo planes, and fighters attacked United States military bases on the island of Oahu, in the territory of Hawaii. The surprise attack on Pearl Harbor killed about three thousand people and destroyed twenty-one U.S. ships. After breaking out in Europe in the late summer of 1939, World War II began for the United States on December 8, 1941, the day after Pearl Harbor, when Congress declared war on Japan. Later, the United States would join the Allies—Great Britain, France, and the Soviet Union—and go to war against Nazi Germany.

Like the armed forces, J. Edgar Hoover and the FBI had not expected the attack. Nevertheless, the

FBI did have a warning. It had come from a spy named Dusko Popov, who had worked in Europe as a double agent. The German government used Popov as a spy, but Popov passed on everything he knew to Germany's enemy, Great Britain. Months before the Japanese attack, Popov was asked by Germany to carry out a very important mission for the Japanese. He was to gather detailed information on Hawaii, including maps and diagrams of Pearl Harbor.

Popov himself had arrived in the United States and had tried to warn the FBI about the Japanese threat to Pearl Harbor. But Hoover did not like or trust foreigners, no matter where their loyalties lay. He especially did not like Popov. Like Hoover, Popov was a bachelor. But unlike Hoover, he led a wild private life. Hoover was strict, and he frowned on Popov's behavior. He did not trust Popov and he did not bother to pass Popov's information on to the military or to the president. As a result, U.S. commanders lacked crucial information that might have prevented the complete surprise that Japan achieved at Pearl Harbor.

Although investigations by Congress and the military spread plenty of blame around for the disaster at Pearl Harbor, the FBI escaped criticism. Popov's actions and reports remained closely guarded secrets. This allowed Popov to keep his cover, but it also allowed Hoover and the bureau to escape any

public knowledge of their inaction. Popov himself returned to Europe in the summer of 1942 to carry on his very dangerous work as a double agent.

Hoover may not have acted on Popov's information, but he had prepared for the war. For several years, he had been drawing up a custodial detention list, which included the names of suspected spies and sympathizers of Japan, Germany, and Italy. Immediately after the bombing of Pearl Harbor, the FBI arrested thousands of these suspects, who were given hearings held by the Justice Department. Although most were released, a few were deported from the country. In addition, a large number of Japanese-Americans were sent to internment camps in California. They would stay there for the duration of the war.

Before the war, the FBI had also set up a language school, which trained its students in German, Italian, Japanese, and Russian, the most important language in the Soviet Union. After graduating, students translated information and intercepted communications from the country's enemies. They infiltrated organizations in the United States suspected of helping the Axis powers. Other informants worked for the FBI in factories and guarded against sabotage. The FBI had its spies in the military, as well.

Hoover intended to make the FBI an important part of the war effort. He asked that members of the FBI be exempted (excused) from the draft. He hired more agents, and put many of them on cases of suspected espionage and sedition. President Roosevelt also put the FBI in charge of wartime censorship. Newspapers, magazines, and book publishers had to send the bureau advance copies of all articles concerning military matters or anything to do with the war. Any information that the Bureau thought should be secret, or that might hinder the war effort, had to be taken out before the article or book could be published.

During World War II, the number of people working for the FBI doubled as the bureau returned to the job that A. Mitchell Palmer and J. Edgar Hoover had undertaken in the early 1920s: gathering information on groups and individuals suspected of opposing the U.S. government.

## Taps and Bugs

Agents of the FBI learned many different ways of gathering information. One of the most useful investigative methods was to place a "tap" on a telephone wire. A wiretap allowed an agent to secretly listen to a private phone conversation. Another method was to place hidden microphones in a room. These "bugs" could be turned on and off,

while a wire delivered the conversation in the room to someone listening close by or at FBI headquarters in Washington.

The FBI placed bugs and taps on thousands of suspects. Agents learned how to break into private homes without being noticed to get the surveillance devices into place and to collect evidence. They also had hotel rooms across the country wired for sound. Telephone conversations as well as telegrams to and from foreign destinations were intercepted and written down. Agents also worked the nation's post offices, where the FBI had mail opened and copied.

There was one problem with taps and bugs—using them was against the law (as was opening private mail). By Section 605 of the Federal Communications Act of 1934, intercepting a private conversation, without permission, was illegal. Such surveillance could not be used in a court as evidence against a suspect. In addition, the attorney general, Robert Jackson, stood firmly against covert surveillance of any kind. In March 1940, Jackson sent written instructions to Hoover that forbade the FBI from using electronic surveillance.

After the war began in Europe, Hoover worked to have the ban ended. He let it be known, to the press and to President Franklin Roosevelt, that Jackson's orders were hindering the FBI in its work of finding foreign spies. Roosevelt agreed, and on May 21, 1940, he gave his personal authorization for Hoover to use bugs and taps whenever Hoover thought them necessary for the purpose of national defense. He also instructed Hoover to use them

**Hoover Opposes the Internment Camps**

Although J. Edgar Hoover fought World War II with enthusiasm, he did not go along with the government program to arrest and intern Japanese citizens. For Hoover, loyalty was not a question of race or nationality.

By Executive Order 9066, signed on February 19, 1942, the Department of Justice was authorized to arrest and imprison one hundred twenty thousand American citizens of Japanese descent. Hoover reacted with a 480-page report, in which he stated,

> [it is] extremely unfortunate that the Government . . .and the public, did, in the past, seize upon what they first believed to be a simple determining factor of loyalty. There actually can be only one efficient method of processing the Japanese for loyalty, which consists of individual, not mass, consideration.[1]

Hoover had another good reason for opposing the internment program. To round up so many citizens would have meant cooperating with other government agencies as well as the U.S. military. Hoover always placed himself in control, and it was a policy throughout his life never to surrender FBI control to any outside agency.

only on aliens, not on U.S. citizens, and only in cases where they were absolutely necessary.

Robert Jackson realized that J. Edgar Hoover had won the battle over surveillance. After the FBI's war on crime during the 1930s, Hoover's standing among the public was high. The Roosevelt administration wanted the FBI and other agencies to use every means possible to win this new and much deadlier war. Still, Jackson did not want any part of it. He asked Hoover not to inform him of surveillance cases. He also wanted Hoover to keep all evidence gathered with taps and bugs in the offices of the FBI. Hoover agreed.

## The Long Island Landing

J. Edgar Hoover still wanted as much good publicity as he could get for his agency, and he did not want any competition from other federal agencies, such as the intelligence arms of the Army and Navy, or the Office of Strategic Services (OSS), a group that collected intelligence in Europe. Hoover found the opportunity to show up his rivals with a spectacular spy case that began on the night of June 13, 1942.

That night, on the Atlantic shores of Long Island, New York, a Coast Guard patrolman named John Cullen found four men dragging a raft onto a beach. The patrolman spoke to the men, but outnumbered, he decided not to try to arrest them. Pretending to believe their story that they were fishermen, he left the beach to notify his superior officer. The next morning, Cullen returned with several armed Coast Guardsmen. They found the beach deserted, except for several partly-hidden crates of explosive devices, German uniforms, and cigarettes.

In the meantime, the four German spies, who had landed by submarine, had disappeared. They wore civilian clothes to disguise themselves and took an ordinary train into New York City. When Hoover learned of the Coast Guard sighting, he immediately ordered a nationwide manhunt by FBI agents.

The manhunt turned out to be unnecessary. The leader of the German group, George Dasch, had orders to commit acts of sabotage against the United States. But Dasch had lived in the United States for twenty years and was not sure of his loyalty to Nazi Germany.

*This FBI poster, with the signature of J. Edgar Hoover, asks for the help of all American citizens in bringing spies and saboteurs to justice.*

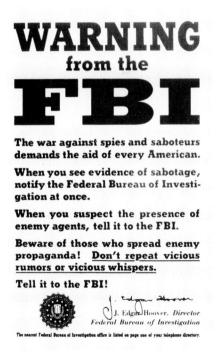

# WARNING
## from the
# FBI

The war against spies and saboteurs demands the aid of every American.

When you see evidence of sabotage, notify the Federal Bureau of Investigation at once.

When you suspect the presence of enemy agents, tell it to the FBI.

Beware of those who spread enemy propaganda! Don't repeat vicious rumors or vicious whispers.

Tell it to the FBI!

J. Edgar Hoover, Director
Federal Bureau of Investigation

The nearest Federal Bureau of Investigation office is listed on page one of your telephone directory.

By the time he arrived in New York he had changed his mind about his mission. He called the FBI's New York office and told his story to the agent in charge.

Not believing Dasch's story, the agent hung up on him. Still determined to reveal himself, Dasch took a train to Washington, where he went straight to FBI headquarters. Several people turned Dasch away. Finally, he managed to see Agent D. M. Ladd, the head of the FBI's Domestic Intelligence Division. After entering Ladd's office, Dasch dumped out $84,000 in cash given to him by the German government to help carry out his mission.

Agents escorted Dasch to the office of the FBI director. Hoover believed his story, and for eight days, the FBI interrogated Dasch on his mission. Dasch gave information on Germany's military and war plans. He also revealed that a second German sabotage mission would soon land on the coast of Florida. More spies would land every six weeks on the Atlantic coast to carry out terror and sabotage attacks.

With the information Dasch supplied, the FBI captured eight German agents. To announce the arrests, Hoover called a press conference on June 27, 1942. The next day, the FBI made national headlines once again—this time not for capturing gangsters, but for foiling the schemes of the Nazi government. Hoover did not, however, reveal exactly how George Dasch had been captured. He did not want the fact that Dasch had turned himself in to come out. Instead, he wanted it to appear that the FBI had solved the spy case of the century. For many years, the public believed just that.

Dasch himself expected to be freed and allowed to remain in the United States. After all, he was the one who had given away the plot and, possibly, saved the United States from a wave of explosions, destruction, and death. However, Dasch and the other seven agents were put on trial. Six of the agents were executed, and Dasch and one other man were given long prison terms. Dasch was later deported.

The case of George Dasch and the Long Island landings went down as a brilliant victory for the FBI. Hoover knew that with such a victory, the public, and the president, would never oppose any methods he could dream up to use against the country's enemies. Taps, bugs, mail openings, and any kind of surveillance, no matter what the law and the constitution might say about them, would be used by the FBI for the duration of the war—and for long afterward.

# 7

# THE HUNT
# FOR
# COMMUNISTS

In May 1945, Germany surrendered, and the war in Europe ended. In August, Japan surrendered after the United States dropped atomic bombs on Hiroshima and Nagasaki, two Japanese cities. World War II had come to a close. The Allies had defeated the Axis powers.

President Roosevelt had died of a stroke on April 12. On the same day, his vice president, Harry Truman, was sworn in as the 33rd president. Truman held to many of Roosevelt's policies, but he did not give much support to J. Edgar Hoover and the FBI. Truman made it clear that J. Edgar Hoover worked for the attorney general and that the FBI was going to be a crime-investigation agency only.

The new president did not go along with break-ins or electronic surveillance of any kind. He did not want the FBI spending its time on suspected radicals or communists. Truman also gave Hoover instructions to report to the attorney general or to the president's aide, Harry Vaughan, if Hoover learned something important.

To J. Edgar Hoover, Truman's orders were a humiliation. But Hoover had his own way of getting revenge. He let Vaughan and other presidential aides know that the FBI was always available if they wanted anyone investigated. Vaughan took Hoover up on the offer. He and other presidential aides often had the FBI carry out investigations of government officials, congressmen, and rivals of the president. Truman did not approve of these investigations, but they were carried out anyway. Hoover knew that if Truman threatened the FBI or Hoover's own job, he could prove that the Truman administration was using the bureau for its own political benefit.

## The Enemies Within

Although the war overseas had ended, Hoover still feared many enemies within the United States. He still saw communism as a dire threat to the country, and he believed that the FBI had to fight against

those who joined or sympathized with the Communist party.

The country, for the most part, supported Hoover in this endeavor. But there were people who did not look favorably on the actions of the FBI. In October 1949, one well-known professor and historian, Bernard DeVoto, stated:

> I say it has gone too far. We are dividing into the hunted and the hunters. There is loose in the United States today the same evil that once split Salem Village between the bewitched and the accused and stole men's reason quite away. We are informers to the secret police. Honest men are spying on their neighbors for patriotism's sake.[1]

As DeVoto feared, the end of World War II had brought the Red Scare back. The war had left only two "superpowers" standing: the United States and the Soviet Union. The two countries were political and economic rivals, and each had other countries as allies. A "cold war" (a period of rivalry but not fighting) developed between the superpowers, while the invention of atomic weapons threatened a devastating war between them.

Congress was taking part in the same fight against communism. During the war, a House Un-American Activities Committee (HUAC) had investigated subversives and communists. The chairman of the committee, Representative Martin Dies of Texas, had great ambitions for the

## The FBI's Public Face

J. Edgar Hoover always took great care that the public saw the best side of the FBI in books, articles, movies, and television shows. Hoover asked, and frequently was given, the chance to review books and scripts before they went into production. The 1959 movie *The FBI Story*, starring James Stewart, was based on a book of the same name, written by Don Whitehead. Both book and movie portrayed the organization as a group of dedicated crime-fighting professionals. It made no mention of wiretapping, burglary, or other activities—some of them illegal—that the agency was carrying on in the fight against Communist subversion.

Hollywood often ran afoul of J. Edgar Hoover, however. The television series *The Untouchables* depicted the federal agent Elliot Ness and his battles against gangsters and bootleggers of the 1920s and 1930s. To keep tabs on this show, Hoover sent members of the FBI's "Crime Research Section" to report on the show and to collect any and all references the scripts made to the FBI. Hoover did not like his old rival Elliot Ness shown as a hero. The FBI director counterattacked with a thorough investigation of the show's producer, Desi Arnaz, who would become the subject of one of the largest FBI files ever collected.

HUAC. He wanted the committee to become a law-enforcement and investigation agency, rivaling the FBI in popularity and influence.

But J. Edgar Hoover did not want any committee competing with the FBI. Nor did he want newspapers and magazines writing about the good work of Martin Dies. He wanted the bureau and J. Edgar Hoover to get all the credit for fighting communists in the United States.

Hoover had the FBI investigate Dies. He also asked for the help of Attorney General Robert Jackson, who cooperated by accusing the Dies committee of interfering with the FBI, then offering Dies a friendly deal: The committee would first check with the Justice Department before bringing any information before the public. In return, the Justice Department would give the committee information on certain people it had investigated. If the Justice Department did not have enough evidence to prosecute these people, the committee could publicize their names and their suspected crimes.

Hoover still wanted to make sure Martin Dies made no trouble for the FBI. To accomplish this, Hoover let Dies know about some information the FBI had gathered. The agency had learned that Dies had received a two thousand dollar bribe from a Jewish refugee during the war. In return for the money, Dies had pushed a law through Congress that allowed the refugee to enter the United States from the island of Cuba.

Dies realized that if the FBI released this information to the press, his political career would be finished. He could not fight the FBI, at least not in public. As a result, he never criticized the bureau, and he made sure to check with the FBI whenever his committee was about to undertake an investigation. Throughout the 1940s and 1950s, and long after Martin Dies left Congress, HUAC and the FBI cooperated very closely.

## Another Red Scare

Hoover suspected that spies in the employ of the Soviet Union were operating in the United States. Their goal was to recruit new members to the Communist party and to undermine the U.S. government. Their most important mission was to

*Fueled by the fear of having his political career destroyed by a bribery charge, Representative Martin Dies made sure that the House Un-American Activities Committee (HUAC) fully cooperated with the FBI.*

steal military secrets, including the plans that allowed U.S. scientists to build the atomic bomb.

The FBI had many informants working in communist circles. One of them, Helen Bentley, was a member of the American Communist Party. She had also worked as a courier for a Soviet spy ring during the war. At some point, she turned against the communists. She decided to tell the FBI the names of her Soviet "handlers," or managers, in the United States.

Hoover knew many of these names, including that of Harry Dexter White, an aide to Treasury Secretary Henry Morgenthau—one of Hoover's rivals. He also knew the name of Alger Hiss, a State Department official who had once been acting secretary general of the United Nations.

Hoover asked the attorney general to allow electronic surveillance of Hiss. The attorney general agreed. The FBI burglarized Hiss's home, tapped his phone, and placed microphones throughout his house. Nevertheless, the microphones and wiretaps captured nothing that would serve as evidence that Hiss was working as a spy.

Hoover had other ways of catching his man. He leaked the information that Hiss was a spy to the press. These leaks served two important purposes: They warned the public that communist spies were living and working in the United States, and they hurt Harry Truman, whose administration came under fire for sheltering suspected foreign agents.

In 1948, as Truman was running for re-election, the FBI arranged for Bentley and a writer named Whittaker Chambers to testify in front of the House Un-American Activities Committee. Before Bentley came forward, Chambers had accused White and Hiss of being communists. In August, Chambers again publicly accused Hiss of being a Soviet spy. In response, Hiss sued Chambers for slandering him.

A member of HUAC, Richard Nixon of California, led the investigation of Alger Hiss. Nixon found the Hiss case to be a difficult one. Chambers often changed his testimony, and he did not seem to be a reliable witness. But in December 1948, Chambers led two HUAC investigators to a pumpkin patch on his Maryland farm. From a hollow pumpkin, he pulled out five rolls of microfilm. On the microfilm, he claimed, were official and secret government documents. Chambers claimed that Hiss had given him these "pumpkin papers."

A trial for espionage resulted from Chambers' testimony. This trial ended with a hung jury—the members could not agree if Hiss was guilty or innocent. But at a second trial, Hiss was convicted and sentenced to ten years in prison. At this trial, his alleged crime was not espionage but perjury (giving

false testimony under oath). Nevertheless, the FBI and HUAC had caught their man.

To many people, Hiss was a victim of an unfair investigation, a "witch hunt" in which certain people were unjustly hunted down and tried, just as certain people were accused and tried for witchcraft in colonial Massachusetts. But to many others, the trial of Alger Hiss seemed to prove that there were indeed Soviet spies working in the United States, and that J. Edgar Hoover was doing his utmost to root them out and put them in jail. The Hiss trial had one more important result: It brought Richard Nixon, a friend of Hoover's and of the FBI, into the limelight.

In 1952, Dwight Eisenhower would select Nixon as his vice-presidential running mate. Hoover supported Eisenhower, and to help his campaign he gathered material on Eisenhower's opponent, Adlai Stevenson. The FBI files indicated that Stevenson and his running mate, Senator Estes Kefauver, had both been in trouble with the law for minor crimes. Hoover managed to pass this information on to Eisenhower supporters in the press. Although the stories were not printed, many people knew about them. The FBI files led to the spreading of rumors about Stevenson and Kefauver that hurt their campaign.

## The Rosenberg Spy Case

Eisenhower and Nixon won the 1952 presidential election. The election represented an important victory for J. Edgar Hoover, who knew that Eisenhower completely supported the work of the FBI. Eisenhower had no doubts about the investigation of communists and subversives in the government. He wanted these investigations to go full speed ahead.

Most Americans supported Eisenhower and Hoover in their fight against the communists. They believed that spies were at work within the United States. Two of those spies, in fact, were sitting on death row, waiting for their execution, as Eisenhower took the oath of office in early 1953.

In 1951, Julius and Ethel Rosenberg had been found guilty of espionage and sentenced to death. Two years earlier, the FBI had discovered that a British scientist, Klaus Fuchs, was passing atomic secrets to the Soviet Union. Fuchs worked in the laboratory at Los Alamos, New Mexico, where the United States designed and built its atomic weapons. He had been hired and paid by Harry Gold, a Soviet agent who was thought to have recruited another Los Alamos worker, David Greenglass, into the spy ring. When Greenglass was interrogated by FBI agents, he claimed that he

had been recruited as a spy by his brother-in-law, Julius Rosenberg.

In July 1950, Julius Rosenberg was arrested. But the FBI could not get Julius to confess to anything. In order to force a confession, the bureau also arrested his wife, Ethel, who went on trial with her husband on March 6, 1951. On the witness stand, the Rosenbergs refused to name any more conspirators. Both denied any involvement in stealing atomic secrets. Nevertheless, Judge Irving Kaufman sentenced the Rosenbergs to death, telling them, "This country is engaged in a life or death struggle with a completely different system . . . who knows but that millions more of innocent people may pay the price of your treason."[2]

Hoover and the FBI felt sure that Julius Rosenberg would confess to save Ethel's life. They offered him a deal: If Rosenberg named other members of the spy ring, the death sentences would be changed to long prison terms. In the meantime, lawyers working for the Rosenbergs appealed their sentence.

Many writers saw the Rosenbergs as victims of a vicious spy hunt. They were caught up in the nationwide fear of communism, and they were being punished for their left-wing political beliefs. Articles appeared in newspapers and magazines, that the death sentence not be carried out. Some writers claimed that the Rosenbergs were innocent, others that the sentence was too harsh—especially since Fuchs, Gold, and Greenglass (who had all confessed) were given prison terms instead of death sentences.

Yet the courts denied all appeals. A few days before the scheduled execution, FBI agents traveled from New York City to the Sing Sing federal prison in upstate New York. The agents waited patiently for a confession, but it never took place. Both Rosenbergs went to the electric chair on June 19, 1953.

## Hoover and McCarthy

The Rosenberg case represented another triumph for the FBI. While Hoover might have had doubts about the guilt of Ethel Rosenberg, he felt little remorse about her death. For Hoover, the Rosenbergs represented a dangerous enemy, one that threatened the entire country, its democratic institutions, and its way of life.

Hoover had a favorite quote: ". . . In 1917 when the Communists overthrew the Russian government there was one Communist for every 2,277 persons in Russia. In the United States today there is one Communist for every 1,814 persons."[3]

Just because the party was small did not mean it was no longer dangerous. It was just as dangerous in the 1950s, Hoover believed, as it had been when he

was fighting it in the 1920s. For this reason, Hoover agreed to set up an entirely new FBI operation, known as COINTELPRO. This acronym stood for "COunter INTELligence PROgram." The bureau used the COINTELPRO program to get inside and disrupt the Communist party. The bureau hired informants to join the party and then make trouble. These FBI operatives spread rumors that certain members were disloyal. They accused other members of being spies and snitches for the government. They started arguments at party meetings. They embarrassed party members by getting their names into local newspapers and getting them fired from their jobs.

Hoover knew that if the COINTELPRO were ever brought to light, it would face little opposition. Many politicians in Washington greatly admired J. Edgar Hoover. They envied his power as well as his popularity. Hoover, they saw, held strong and unbending beliefs. He was a patriot and a crime-fighter, and he was as skillful a politician as any of them. For thirty years, he had used the issue of communism to protect his job and gain favor with presidents and attorneys general.

In the 1950s, many senators and representatives tried to show themselves as tough on communism as J. Edgar Hoover. In their speeches and writings, politicians declared themselves firmly on the side of the spy hunters. Many campaigned, and won, on this theme. Committees were set up in the House and Senate to root out the enemy within. The House of Representatives had the House Un-American Activities Committee. The Senate had the Permanent Investigations Subcommittee of the Committee on Government Operations. Its leader was Senator Joseph McCarthy of Wisconsin.

An outspoken, tough, and ambitious politician, McCarthy was best known for accusing people of being communists. From time to time, he would produce a list of names, wave it in the air, and declare that he had discovered another group of spies. There were spies in government agencies, McCarthy said, spies in the State Department, spies in the U.S. Congress, even spies in the Defense Department. The accusations brought scandals, large headlines in the newspapers, and embarrassment, especially to McCarthy's political enemies.

Hoover and McCarthy worked together for several years. Hoover sent FBI reports on suspected communists to McCarthy. The McCarthy committee would then start an investigation. The work of the committee took place in public, before spectators and reporters. The suspects McCarthy named suffered public suspicion and ridicule. Many of them saw their careers destroyed, merely on the suspicion of sympathizing with communists.

In the early 1950s, McCarthy's methods served Hoover well. Many FBI targets could not be brought to trial because of faulty evidence. Rumors of sympathy for communism were not enough to convict somebody of treason. Writing and speeches, no matter how rebellious, were protected by the Constitution. Electronic surveillance, such as wiretaps, room bugs, and material gathered during a burglary, was illegal. It could never be used by a prosecutor at trial. But if Senator McCarthy revealed the names of these FBI targets, even if giving no evidence whatsoever, these suspects could be ruined all the same.

Eventually, McCarthy went too far. Soon after President Eisenhower took office, the McCarthy committee began making accusations against the new administration. McCarthy himself accused the president of being soft on communism. Hoover began to worry. He knew that senators came and went, but that the bureau and his own office must remain open for business. His first loyalty belonged to the bureau and to the man who assured his job: the president.

In early 1954, McCarthy began making accusations of spying within the United States Army. The Senate held hearings on the matter in April 1954. The entire nation watched closely—the hearings were the first ever to be held in front of television cameras.

At the hearings, McCarthy again accused the Army of sheltering spies and of trying to block his investigation. To support his case, he held up a two-page letter that he claimed J. Edgar Hoover had written to him. The letter, which had a typewritten signature, contained the names of suspected communists within the Army. Senator Thomas Welch, one of McCarthy's opponents, objected to the letter and challenged McCarthy to prove it was genuine. The cameras swung toward J. Edgar Hoover.

Hoover carefully prepared his answer. He claimed that Senator McCarthy's letter had not come to him from the FBI. Instead, it contained seven paragraphs of a report that Hoover had prepared in 1951 and had sent to the United States Army. Somehow, McCarthy's staff had intercepted the report, and now the senator was using it to slander the military on national television.

Hoover's statement made McCarthy look like a liar. From that point, it was downhill for Senator McCarthy and his committee. The Army-McCarthy hearings quickly ended. His fellow senators sharply criticized him and his anti-communist witch hunt. His political career destroyed, he died in 1957 from cirrhosis of the liver brought on by heavy drinking.

J. Edgar Hoover played a crucial role in McCarthy's career. He had helped the senator to achieve fame and power. He had also brought

## HUAC and Hollywood

One of the most useful tools of the House Un-American Activities Committee was the threat of an investigation and a "blacklist" that would prevent film writers, actors, and directors from getting work. By using this threat, HUAC got support and sometimes cooperation in their investigations.

The actor Burt Lancaster provides one example. During the early 1950s, Lancaster often spoke out against HUAC and the hunt for communists. He worked with blacklisted movie actors, ignoring HUAC's official disapproval. Then he saw the committee directly threaten his own movie career. In 1954, the government restricted a passport he needed for travel to Mexico to make a movie. Then, in 1956, the government threatened to deny him the passport he needed to travel to France, where he was scheduled to work on the movie *Trapeze*.

Lancaster then wrote an affidavit supporting the work of HUAC. "I am completely opposed to anyone who is a member of the Communist Party [sic] or who is a Communist Party or who is a Communist sympathizer in the United States today," he wrote in his pro-HUAC affidavit. "If I knew such a person I would feel it my obligation to report him or her to the appropriate investigative agencies."[4]

*At first, Hoover supported Senator Joseph McCarthy. However, after McCarthy started to make accusations toward the Eisenhower administration and the military, Hoover worked to discredit him.*

McCarthy down. He would not help McCarthy attack the United States Army or the Eisenhower administration. For Hoover, these two institutions had to be protected against attacks from outsiders.

## The Hoover Bureau

To J. Edgar Hoover, President Eisenhower represented solid, traditional American values. These values had been instilled in Hoover by his mother and by his upbringing in a respectable, middle-class Washington, D.C., neighborhood. Eisenhower had been a general, the man who won the war in Europe.

Hoover also saw himself as a soldier. In his own mind, he was fighting a patriotic battle to uphold traditional values in the government and especially within the FBI.

Hoover realized, as did many people, that the Great Depression and World War II had brought drastic changes to American society. The United States had become an urban, industrialized society, and its people were more mobile and restless than ever before. To people of Hoover's generation, this modernization was bringing the old institutions of church, school, and family under attack. As his family's youngest member—the "runt of the litter"—and as a short and stuttering high-school student, Hoover had grown up fighting. Even after achieving his life's ambition to become director of the bureau, he remained a combative individual. He saw himself as a valiant fighter in a deadly, never-ending contest of good and evil.

By the 1950s, he could claim one very important victory: mastery of the FBI. Although it was a publicly funded federal agency, the bureau in many ways personally belonged to J. Edgar Hoover. He had built the FBI to fit his idea of what a well-run inves-tigative agency should be. Nobody knew this better than Hoover's "special agents." The agents learned the Hoover philosophy from the day they started training. They were to dress a certain way, cut their hair short, and always wear hats (even though hats, by the 1950s, were going out of style). The bureau kept watch on their personal lives and even had to approve their marriages. The agents had to weigh a certain amount, depending on their height. They also had important letter-writing responsibilities, as Hoover appreciated support and flattery from his employees. One FBI leader, William Sullivan, put it like this:

> If you want to progress in the Bureau, if you want a good assignment instead of being bounced around from one office to the other, you better do what these others do and write these flattering letters.
>
> . . . He [Hoover] just loved to get these letters. You just couldn't praise him too much; you couldn't be too lavish in telling him what a great job he was doing for the country. [5]

FBI agents knew that ignoring the director, making the bureau look bad, or going against the rules would bring severe punishment. They could be sent to a distant, out-of-the-way FBI office, where there was little to do.

*Hoover takes aim at a target in an FBI shooting range where agents trained every day.*

Unlike most federal workers, they could also be fired on the spot and for no particular reason. Because their pay was good, and because they also earned good pensions, agents went along with the rules.

Hoover followed certain strict rules as well. His private life went like clockwork. He woke up at a certain time, went to work at a certain time. He provided detailed menus for his cook at home, and he always ate lunch at the same restaurant in Washington, D.C. Twice a year, he took vacations—always to Florida in the winter, and always to California in the summer. He kept the same secretary, Helen Gandy, from the 1920s to the 1970s. He kept the same maid, cook, chauffeur, and gardener for decades. In his lifetime, he lived in only two houses: his boyhood home on Seward Square and, after his mother died, in a large house on 30th Place, in northwest Washington.

Inside this new home, Hoover kept the same tidiness and order he had known as a boy on Seward Square. He collected hundreds of antiques and art objects, assigning each a certain place inside the house that never changed, in some cases over decades. The furniture in his living room and bedroom was never moved. The rugs and carpets were kept straight and spotless. All the pictures hung at a certain height.

Hoover was a precise and careful man, but he was also a loyal friend—especially to Clyde Tolson. Hoover had met Tolson in the 1920s and had hired him for the Bureau of Investigation. Tolson quickly rose within the ranks to become the second-in-command at the FBI. He and Hoover worked together, ate lunch together, and took vacations together. J. Edgar Hoover never married and had no family. In many ways, Clyde Tolson was J. Edgar Hoover's family.

## A Positive Image

Hoover had little reason to doubt his beliefs or his work in the 1950s. During this decade, the FBI became the most powerful agency in the entire federal government. The president, and most of the people, supported it, as they always had. Hoover worked hard to keep up the positive image of the FBI and put its good work in the newspaper headlines. He wanted the public to see the FBI as an organization of brave and skillful men, fighting against dangerous criminals and spies.

An entire FBI department, the Crime Records Unit, was set up to feed the positive image of the Bureau. The members of Crime Records wrote and sent out stories on the FBI for newspapers to run. They gave information to writers working on FBI stories. They reviewed scripts for movies, radio

broadcasts, and television shows. They kept track of newspapers and magazines that supported the FBI, and those that did not. Anybody criticizing or doubting the work of the Bureau was put on a "No Contact" list. They would get no information and no cooperation whatsoever from the FBI.

The members of Crime Records even wrote books. One FBI-written book, *Masters of Deceit*, appeared in 1958. The book discussed the evils and the threat of communism. Although J. Edgar Hoover's name appeared on the title page, Hoover did not write *Masters of Deceit*. Instead, he simply reviewed chapters written by the members of Crime Records. *Masters of Deceit* appeared in hardcover and paperback editions and quickly became one of the biggest best-sellers of 1958.

## The Mafia and J. Edgar Hoover

In many ways, Hoover had changed the work of the FBI since the 1930s, when his G-men fought against gangsters, bank robbers, and other miscreants. The enemies now were the Soviet Union and commu-nism—but crime of a more ordinary sort still existed.

There had been large, organized criminal gangs working in the United States for decades. Many of these gangs started during Prohibition, in the 1920s. They supplied illegal beer and liquor. After Prohibition, they survived by controlling illegal activities in many large cities. They paid bribes to police departments to look the other way. They controlled labor unions, made loans, ran gambling operations, and blackmailed ordinary businesses. Many of the gangs were run by small groups of criminals, many of them of Italian descent, and together these Italian gangs were known to the public as the Mafia.

J. Edgar Hoover had done little to fight the Mafia. For reasons of his own, he had sometimes even denied that the Mafia existed. He knew that to fight this group, he would have to cooperate with other government departments, such as the rest of the Justice Department. He did not want to do this—he wanted to keep the FBI completely independent. He also did not want FBI agents getting involved in organized crime investigations. He believed this was a job for local police departments. He feared the chance of his agents taking bribes and being corrupted. This had happened to many federal agents and police chiefs working against the Mafia.

Hoover's attitude changed on November 14, 1957. On that day, police in upstate New York arrested dozens of Mafia leaders who were meeting in the small town of Apalachin, New York. Newspapers across the country ran the story in bold headlines. Most people had suspected that

organized crime existed, although they could not be sure. The "Apalachin Conference" proved that the Mafia was bigger and more real than anyone had imagined.

The Apalachin Conference also made the FBI look incompetent. The bureau had done little or nothing about organized crime for many years. Hoover could no longer deny that organized crime existed. He ordered the bureau to set up a new department. The Special Investigations Division took control of Mafia investigations. The FBI also began covert surveillance of organized crime. In 1959, the FBI began bugging meetings of Mafia leaders in one of their Chicago hideouts. From this bug came detailed information on nearly every organized crime leader in the country.

In this effort, Hoover's emphasis on scientific methods and new technology paid off. The Mafia investigations proved to be a great success. From the late 1950s on, Hoover and his staff had detailed knowledge of the workings of organized crime and, when necessary, could shine a bright light on the activities of Mafia leaders.

# 8

# THE 1960s

Hoover had built the FBI into one of the most trusted agencies of the federal government. He had reason for satisfaction—but he had good reason to worry as well. A new decade had begun, and his favorite president, Dwight Eisenhower, would have to step down, after having served two terms. A new president was coming, and although Hoover threw all of his support behind Richard M. Nixon, he still could not guarantee Nixon's election.

The fight against communism was not going well, either. Although the FBI kept up its work of tracking and investigating subversives, the anticommunist fever in the House and Senate was dying down. Senator Joseph McCarthy had died in 1957. Many

politicians were criticizing the work of the House Un-American Activities Committee. And on May 12, 1960, thousands of students demonstrated in San Francisco against HUAC and its investigations. This would be the first of many demonstrations to come during the 1960s.

The nation had new concerns and wanted new leadership. John F. Kennedy, a democratic congressman from Massachusetts, symbolized the trend. To the voters, Kennedy represented the new generation and a clean break with the problems and old-fashioned prejudices of the past. He defeated Nixon in the presidential election of 1960.

## The Kennedy Files

Hoover and the FBI already had a very thick file on John F. Kennedy. He was the son of Joseph Kennedy, a former bootlegger, businessman, and ambassador who headed one of the wealthiest families in the nation. During World War II, John Kennedy had served as a naval officer. He had commanded a PT boat in the South Pacific and had been seriously injured in battle. The voters looked on Kennedy as a courageous young war hero.

But Kennedy had also come under investigation for some unheroic activities. During the war, FBI agents had kept a close watch on his friendship with a young Danish woman named Inga Arvad. She was glamorous and beautiful—but she had also been close to several important leaders in Nazi Germany, including the Nazi leader Adolf Hitler. The FBI suspected her of being a German spy.

Hoover knew this investigation very well, and he also let John Kennedy know about it. If the public found out about his relationship with Inga Arvad, Kennedy's political career would be over. He would look like a fool and a traitor to his country. Only Hoover could make this story public, and only Hoover could keep it a secret. Just a few days after Kennedy was sworn in as president, he reappointed Hoover as the director of the FBI.

## The Kennedy Brothers

John F. Kennedy had several reasons for reappointing J. Edgar Hoover. He may have been worried about the FBI file on him, but he was also concerned about his standing among the voters. The election of 1960 had been very, very close. Kennedy knew Hoover had the support of many people for his fight against the communists. By reappointing Hoover, he protected himself from his own past and won support from the anticommunists as well.

But Hoover did not feel comfortable with John Kennedy. The president was twenty-two years younger than Hoover, and his politics and personal demeanor were very different from that of the

director of the FBI. Hoover grew even more uncomfortable when John appointed his younger brother, Robert Kennedy, as attorney general—Hoover's boss.

Robert Kennedy dressed informally. He wore no jacket, and sometimes no tie. He kept his hair long, and he never wore a hat. He would never have met the FBI dress code. Worse, he often dropped in on Hoover unannounced and brought his family dog to the Justice Department building, which was against regulations. Everything he did, and everything about him—especially his youth—irritated Hoover.

President Kennedy also ended the director's close contact with the White House, which had always been a source of pride to J. Edgar Hoover. The president asked Hoover to report to his brother and not to the White House. A direct telephone line was installed from Robert Kennedy's office to Hoover's FBI office. If Hoover had something to report, he was supposed to send it to Robert Kennedy first. Hoover was humiliated.

Under Robert Kennedy, the Justice Department also changed in ways that did not suit the FBI director. Robert Kennedy had two big priorities for the members of his department and, he thought, for the FBI. One was organized crime. The other was civil rights.

## Hoover and the Civil Rights Movement

The issue of civil rights for African Americans gained national attention in the middle of the 1950s, a time when J. Edgar Hoover and the FBI kept busy fighting communism. For many years, African Americans had endured second-class status throughout the United States, particularly in the South. African Americans had to use separate facilities in public places, where signs for "Colored Only" showed the way to separate bathrooms, separate doors, separate drinking fountains, and separate places on public transportation. African-American students studied in segregated schools, where the races did not mix.

In 1955, an African-American woman, Rosa Parks, challenged the segregation laws. She had refused to give up her seat to a white man on a Montgomery, Alabama, bus. This led to a boycott, in which African Americans refused to ride the buses and which quickly sparked a confrontation between whites and blacks. The leader of the boycott was a young minister named Martin Luther King, Jr.

Eventually, Congress passed new laws against segregation. A Supreme Court decision in 1964 ended segregation in public schools. But new laws and court decisions could not, by themselves, desegregate the South. Many white citizens, and most

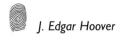 

white leaders, resisted them and fought against any actions that would give the races equality.

The Montgomery bus boycott was just the beginning for the civil rights movement. Many more boycotts, marches, and speeches took place. In some places, riots and fights broke out. Police battled African-American demonstrators with nightsticks, attack dogs, and fire hoses.

The troubles grew worse in the early 1960s, during the Kennedy administration. John and Robert Kennedy supported the civil rights laws and desegregation. Attorney General Robert Kennedy wanted the FBI to help make sure the South observed the civil rights laws.

But J. Edgar Hoover held a very low opinion of the civil rights movement. He did not believe Rosa Parks or anyone else should disobey the laws, no matter how unfair they seemed. He opposed public demonstrations and "civil disobedience" of any kind. To Hoover, public disorder seemed a much greater threat to the nation than segregation laws.

Hoover was not open-minded when it came to recognizing equality between the races and did not feel that any law or court decision would change things. The only African-American FBI employees were those who served the director personally as chauffeurs, bodyguards, house servants, doormen, and gardeners. One of Hoover's top aides, William C. Sullivan, recalls:

> Our agents had infiltrated the civil rights movement to see if the civil rights workers were part of a subversive plot to overthrow the United States, but they [the FBI agents] had kept out of the way of the local white citizens who were making life so dangerous for these civil rights workers. This was in part because Hoover didn't want to offend the southern sheriffs and police chiefs who had helped the bureau solve so many cases in the past. He also felt more comfortable and more sympathetic toward these old rednecks than he did toward blacks and students, whose motivations and lifestyles he didn't understand at all.[1]

Hoover also did not believe enforcing civil rights was the job of the FBI. Instead, he believed the FBI's most important task was to continue the fight against communism. He even believed communists were infecting the civil rights movement, and felt sure they were trying to influence Martin Luther King, Jr., and other civil rights leaders. In Hoover's view, the communists were trying to use the civil rights movement to overthrow the democratic system.

Hoover also had two very practical reasons for keeping the FBI uninvolved in the South and civil rights. First, he did not want the FBI cooperating with Robert Kennedy's Justice Department. He wanted the bureau to remain a completely independent agency under his personal direction.

Second, Hoover did not like failure. When FBI agents investigated a civil rights case, and someone was brought to trial for violating the law, the juries of the South—made up of whites only—rarely passed a guilty verdict. In the area of civil rights, the bureau seemed to be spending its time, money, and energy for nothing.

## The Bureau in the South

The civil rights movement picked up energy in the early 1960s. In 1961, a group of black and white "Freedom Riders" tried to force the integration of buses and bus depots. These Freedom Riders were mobbed and beaten in several southern towns. Robert Kennedy ordered federal marshals to protect them.

In the fall of 1961, an African-American student named James Meredith attempted to enroll at the University of Mississippi. Hostile white students and local police met him at the front doors to prevent the university's integration. The National Guard was called out to stop the fighting. The same thing happened at the University of Alabama in 1963. In the meantime, white students from the north were traveling south to help African Americans. The violence grew worse.

The Justice Department and Robert Kennedy pressured Hoover to get the FBI involved. Hoover agreed, but not to stop the violence or to fight segregation. Instead, Hoover ordered agents to begin surveillance on Martin Luther King, Jr., and on several of King's aides. Hoover felt certain that Communists were working in King's organization, the Southern Christian Leadership Conference (SCLC).

Hoover felt a great fear and suspicion of Martin Luther King, Jr. He ordered his agents to bug hotel rooms and apartments where King stayed and place wiretaps on SCLC telephones. The FBI file on Martin Luther King, Jr., grew very thick with evidence—recorded conversations, opened mail, photographs, and other information—that Hoover knew he could use against King if necessary.

Hoover also worked on Robert Kennedy. He sent evidence to Kennedy that, Hoover believed, proved that the communists were infiltrating the SCLC. Kennedy read and listened to the evidence. He began to have his own doubts about the civil rights movement. In October 1963, he agreed to allow FBI wiretaps on King's home and office. Kennedy wanted the wiretapping to remain a secret, however. Such activity, he knew, was illegal. The law only allowed secret wiretapping if the target posed a threat to national security.

For Hoover, this action served a dual purpose. He could gather evidence that might harm Martin Luther King, Jr., and he could prove that Robert

Kennedy had allowed him to do so. Kennedy had a reputation for supporting civil rights. If the public found out that he was allowing the FBI to wiretap Martin Luther King, Jr., his reputation would suffer. His supporters would abandon him, and the voters might turn away from John F. Kennedy and the Democratic party.

## Death of a President

Although J. Edgar Hoover worked all his life at FBI headquarters in Washington, D. C., the FBI was much more than a few floors of a big building in the nation's capital. The agents of the FBI worked at local bureaus in major cities throughout the country. Each agent dealt with hundreds of cases, large and small: murders, kidnappings, counterfeiting, robberies, transportation of stolen goods, and illegal gambling, as well as fraud and other kinds of "white-collar crime." FBI investigations could take a few days or many years, while agents gathered and analyzed enough evidence to bring a suspect to trial.

Every day, FBI agents came into contact with the underside of ordinary life. They met criminals of all kinds. They often heard threats against their lives. They made arrests and took dangerous risks. And they did not always have to leave the office. Sometimes the criminals came to them.

One day in late 1963, a short and slight man by the name of Lee Harvey Oswald appeared at the FBI office in Dallas, Texas. Oswald was angry—angry enough to threaten to blow up the Dallas office and all the agents working there. The Dallas agents knew about Oswald, as they had already interviewed him. Oswald had lived in the Soviet Union and was suspected of being a communist. He had married a Russian woman and brought her to the United States. FBI agent James Hosty had interviewed Marina Oswald, too, and that interview was what had angered Oswald.

However, the FBI took no special notice of Oswald. To Agent Hosty, Oswald seemed hostile but not especially dangerous or important. There were no serious charges to bring against him. The FBI did not bother to tap his phone or bug his home. They did not put him on the detention lists of people to be jailed in case of war with the Soviet Union.

Hosty read the note Oswald brought to his office. The note threatened to blow up the Dallas Police Department and the FBI office. Hosty filed the note away.

On November 22, 1963, in downtown Dallas, Oswald climbed to the sixth floor of the Texas School Book Depository, where he worked. He aimed a high-powered rifle out the window. From

his perch, he shot and killed John F. Kennedy as the
president rode past the building in a motorcade.

The assassination shocked the nation, and
especially the agents of the FBI. They had never
taken Oswald seriously enough to take him into
custody or bring charges against him. They had paid
little attention to his threatening note. Now, he had
murdered the president.

Soon after the assassination, Oswald was shot
and killed while in police custody. The public and
the leaders of Congress searched for someone else to
blame for the assassination. The spotlight began to
shine on the FBI and its Dallas office. In the meantime, James Hosty had destroyed Oswald's note.

Many people began to suspect some kind of
conspiracy in the Kennedy assassination. Many also
wondered why the FBI had failed to stop it. Oswald
was known to have had ties with the Communist
party. Yet he had given the slip to Agent Hosty and
others in the bureau.

Hoover knew he had to do something to bring the
situation under control. The reputation of his bureau
was at stake. He began working on a secret report to
Lyndon B. Johnson, Kennedy's vice president.

Johnson, who was sworn in as the 36th president
immediately after the assassination, was deathly
afraid of a conspiracy. He thought the Mafia, or the
Cuban leader Fidel Castro, or some other Kennedy

enemy had used Oswald to kill the president. The same conspirators may have planned the murder of Lee Harvey Oswald to cover up the plot.

Johnson had asked Hoover to dig deep and give him the truth about the killing. But Hoover's report stated there was no conspiracy behind the Kennedy assassination. Hoover reported that Lee Harvey Oswald was a deranged individual who had acted alone.

A congressional committee met to investigate President Kennedy's assassination. The head of the committee was Earl Warren, a Supreme Court justice. The Warren Commission relied on FBI reports supplied by J. Edgar Hoover. The commission came to the same conclusion as Hoover: Lee Harvey Oswald had acted alone, and there had been no conspiracy to assassinate President Kennedy.

## The Johnson Years

Lyndon B. Johnson and J. Edgar Hoover had known each other for a long time. For many years they had been neighbors on the same block in northwest Washington, D. C., and they also considered themselves friends. Hoover felt strong sympathy for Johnson. He was a strong-willed, stubborn, and ambitious politician from Texas, and Hoover appreciated such men. He had another important thing in

common with Johnson: The new president did not get along with Attorney General Robert Kennedy.

Johnson knew that Hoover would prove to be a strong ally for him. He returned the favor by allowing Hoover to remain in his job even though, when he reached the age of seventy, the law required Hoover to retire. Johnson even held a special ceremony for Hoover at the White House. The president announced that he was waiving Hoover's mandatory retirement and remarked:

> J. Edgar Hoover has served the government since 1917—he has served nine Presidents, and this Sunday, he celebrates his fortieth year as Director of the FBI. Under his guiding hand, the FBI has become the greatest investigation body in history.

*President Lyndon Johnson (right) and Hoover were both friends and political allies.*

Edgar, the law says that you must retire next January when you reach your seventieth birthday, and I know you wouldn't want to break the law.

But the nation cannot afford to lose you.[2]

As he had been doing for decades, Hoover used the FBI to collect information on Johnson's political rivals. He also began to ignore Robert Kennedy, who remained attorney general after his brother's death. Whenever he had a special request to make, or an issue to discuss, Hoover went over Kennedy's head and directly to President Johnson.

Johnson had many tough issues to deal with. The country was growing more divided over civil rights. Students were demonstrating for civil rights and against the police and the federal government. The nation was slowly but surely being dragged into a war in distant Vietnam, against the armies of Communist North Vietnam.

## Fighting the Klan

During the Johnson presidency, the FBI and the Justice Department held very different stands on the issue of antiwar protests. While the FBI continued its covert operations, the Justice Department tried to negotiate with student radicals and others opposed to the war. The FBI began new COINTELPRO operations against the Black Panthers, a group of militant African Americans, and against the

Students for a Democratic Society (SDS), a student antiwar group.

Hoover also ordered a COINTELPRO operation against the Ku Klux Klan. The Klan, which dated back to the nineteenth century, had been founded by Confederate officers just after the Civil War. Its original goal was to restore the glory and honor of the South after the humiliating defeat by the Union. By the middle of the twentieth century, the Klan had become a racist hate group whose white members fought against civil rights and integration. Hooded Klan members marched in parades, burned crosses on hillsides, and attacked African Americans in the south.

He may have resisted the civil rights movement, but J. Edgar Hoover had no problem fighting the Ku Klux Klan as well. To Hoover, the Klan represented disorder and defiance of the law, two qualities he could not abide in any organization. And even in the South, the Klan was none too popular among ordinary people. The FBI would win favorable public notice for this effort. It would not be difficult to bring Klan members to trial and to win convictions against them.

To fight the Klan, the FBI recruited informants among its members. These informants disrupted the Klan by starting bitter arguments and inciting suspicion between Klan leaders and followers. They also gave the local police information on when, and where, Klan raids and attacks would take place. In March 1965, when Klan members murdered a civil rights activist named Viola Liuzzo, the FBI solved the crime immediately, scoring a significant victory for the bureau. The COINTELPRO operation turned many Klan groups into bickering, ineffective local groups, which many members eventually left altogether.

Hoover himself still worked against civil rights in his own way. He continued the surveillance of Martin Luther King, Jr. When King was nominated for the Nobel Peace Prize in 1964, Hoover exploded

*On December 1, 1964, Dr. Martin Luther King, Jr., actually went to the FBI offices to meet with Hoover and discuss the director's strong remarks against King.*

in anger. He began a campaign to slander King's name among people who supported him. He released tapes of King's private conversations and private activities. The tapes worried many of King's aides and disrupted the activities of the SCLC. FBI agents sent a threatening letter to King, promising to expose his private actions if he did not disappear from public life.

The FBI operations against King ended in April 1968, when King was shot and killed at a motel in Memphis, Tennessee. The FBI eventually solved this murder, arresting a bank-robber named James Earl Ray for the crime.

Despite the FBI's fight against radicals, Black Panthers, and others opposed by Johnson and Hoover, the country's troubles continued. Deadly riots erupted in Detroit, Los Angeles, Newark, and other cities. Students continued their demonstrations against the war. Militant Black Panthers fought against the institutions Hoover held dear. There seemed little hope of turning back the angry tide, or of winning the war in Vietnam. Frustrated by these problems, Lyndon B. Johnson decided not to run for president in 1968. That fall, Republican Richard Nixon defeated Democrat Hubert Humphrey. J. Edgar Hoover's old ally from the House Un-American Activities Committee had become the 37th president of the United States.

## Director Hoover and President Nixon

Hoover and Nixon had been close allies for a long time. Hoover had helped Nixon in the early 1950s, when Nixon investigated Alger Hiss and other suspected communists in the government. Through the 1950s, Hoover gave Nixon access to FBI reports and information on Nixon's enemies. When he took office as president, Nixon returned the favor. He told Hoover that the Director would have complete support of his White House staff.

The FBI, however, was coming under fire, as was the entire federal government. Civil rights leaders attacked the bureau for its inaction in their fight against segregation. Students were demonstrating for civil rights and against the war in Vietnam. Hoover and Nixon saw the demonstrations as a dire threat. They believed these demonstrating students were tearing down the country and its institutions. To fight back, Hoover ordered a COINTELPRO operation against the Students for a Democratic Society.

## Stopping the Leaks

Nixon believed the United States could win the war in Vietnam. In March 1969, he ordered the bombing of enemy bases and supply roads in Cambodia, a country that neighbored Vietnam. The administration believed the bombing of Cambodia would help the U.S. military win the war. But the bombing had a

stronger effect within the United States. Spreading the war to Cambodia made it all the more unpopular at home.

Nixon saw his popularity decline. It turned out that several newspapers had known much more than they should have about the bombing of Cambodia. Reporters on television and in the newspapers were talking about the administration's war plans. Nixon began to suspect that members of his own administration were sabotaging the war effort. Somebody was leaking his secret plans and information to the press. Nixon was determined to catch the leakers. He asked the FBI to help.

Attorney General John Mitchell authorized Hoover to place wiretaps. The FBI placed a total of seventeen wiretaps on individuals suspected of leaking information or receiving leaked information from government sources. The targets included journalists as well as members of the White House staff and the Department of Defense.

The wiretapping greatly worried J. Edgar Hoover. He had once used such surveillance to catch gangsters and suspected communists. Now he was using it for political purposes. President Nixon simply wanted to catch the people he suspected of opposing him. National security, or the fight against communism, did not seem to be involved.

Hoover knew the wiretaps were illegal even though Nixon often encouraged electronic surveillance of any kind. Hoover's own attitude, however, was changing. He kept the information gathered from the wiretaps separate from the ordinary FBI files. If anyone found out about the illegal wiretapping, his bureau would be in trouble, and he might well have to take the blame and resign. Hoover was growing old, and he was thinking about his legacy—how people would see him and his bureau after his death.

Meanwhile, the antiwar demonstrations grew more violent. On May 4, 1970, members of a National Guard unit shot and killed four students at Kent State University, in Ohio. The killings shocked the public. The government seemed to be running amok, attacking its own people. But Hoover did not see it that way. He strongly opposed antiwar activity of any kind. He saw antiwar demonstrators as traitors to their country. In his opinion, the dead students at Kent State got what they deserved.[3]

## The Legacy of the FBI

President Nixon, meanwhile, was growing very impatient with J. Edgar Hoover. He did not appreciate Hoover's attitude about wiretapping. He began to see his old ally as old-fashioned, an aging dinosaur who was no longer useful.[4]

Nixon and Attorney General John Mitchell demanded more cooperation from Hoover and the FBI. But J. Edgar Hoover had been around Washington far longer than President Nixon. He opposed Nixon's requests for more wiretapping and surveillance.

Unsatisfied, Nixon asked for a complete reorganization of intelligence agencies. He wanted the FBI to cooperate with the Central Intelligence Agency (CIA), the Defense Department, and other departments. These agencies would combine all of the information they had on antiwar protesters, suspected communists, and opponents of any kind. They would submit the information to the White House. Nixon's own staff members would direct intelligence operations: wiretapping, mail opening, informants, burglaries, COINTELPRO operations, and the like.

Hoover let it be known that he strongly opposed this plan. He did not want to be responsible for any more illegal activities. He did not even want to know about them. From now on, Hoover said, the attorney general would have to approve all requests for undercover operations and surveillance. Instead of taking control of such operations, as in the past, Hoover gave up control entirely.

## The Media Break-In

J. Edgar Hoover still believed that antiwar activists should be followed and, if possible, prosecuted. He went before a congressional committee in November 1970. He leaked information to the committee about a conspiracy against the federal government. The ringleaders, he claimed, were planning to blow up the electrical grid of Washington, D.C. They would kidnap Henry Kissinger, the head of the National Security Agency, and demand an end to the bombing in Vietnam as a ransom.

Hoover named the conspirators: two radical priests, Daniel and Philip Berrigan, and a Catholic nun, Sister Elizabeth McAlister. The three were arrested on January 12, 1971. But the FBI actually had little evidence against them. The prosecution failed to convince a jury of their guilt. Hoover had publicly failed—and several members of Congress began demanding his resignation.

Hoover began to realize that keeping secrets could be dangerous. The FBI files showed not only what suspects were doing, but also what the FBI was doing. They contained evidence that could seriously damage the bureau and its fight against crime and subversives. Hoover worried more and more about the files, the illegal surveillance, and public opinion.

Hoover feared that determined FBI opponents were trying to embarrass the bureau. He turned out to be right. On March 8, 1971, burglars broke into the FBI office in Media, Pennsylvania. The thieves made off with armloads of secret FBI files. The

files held information on antiwar activities in Philadelphia, Pennsylvania, and on local college campuses. Over the next several weeks, the files were released, one by one, to the press.

The Media break-in seriously embarrassed the FBI and J. Edgar Hoover. The published files revealed that the bureau was following dozens of campus activists, planting informants, and carrying out illegal activities. For the first time, the public learned about the COINTELPRO actions, as well as FBI burglaries, wiretapping, and bugging. In the opinion of many, Hoover's FBI was running out of control.

## The Pentagon Papers and the Plumbers

President Nixon had worries of his own. The leaks to the press were continuing. Much to the president's embarrassment, a secret Pentagon report on Vietnam was published on June 13, 1971, in *The New York Times*.

Angered by this leak, Nixon demanded a thorough investigation. The FBI agreed, but produced only one suspect, a former Pentagon official named Daniel Ellsberg. Although he had once supported the war, Ellsberg had turned strongly against it. By coincidence, Ellsberg's father-in-law was a friend of J. Edgar Hoover.

Nixon felt certain that a much larger conspiracy against him existed. He also suspected Hoover of going easy on Ellsberg. Frustrated and determined, Nixon set up his own White House investigation unit. He ordered this group to use any and all methods necessary to stop leaks to the press. Because their job was to stop press leaks, the members of the group were known as the Plumbers.

The Plumbers became Nixon's private and secret White House FBI. They were used not only to stop leaks, but to carry out illegal operations against Nixon's enemies. During the presidential campaign of 1972, one of the Plumbers, a former FBI agent named G. Gordon Liddy, arranged a burglary of the offices of the Democratic National Committee, at the Watergate hotel in Washington, D.C.

That fall, Nixon was reelected. But news of the Watergate break-in became public through a series of articles in the *Washington Post*. The articles touched off a

*Former FBI agent G. Gordon Liddy was a member of a secret White House group called the Plumbers, created by President Richard Nixon to do the dirty work that Hoover would not allow his FBI to be a part of.*

scandal that grew worse when Congress began a series of public hearings on the matter. One by one, President Nixon's aides appeared on national television, describing the secretive activities. Eventually, the Watergate scandal would force Nixon to resign from office.

In the meantime, Nixon's opinion of J. Edgar Hoover had fallen to a new low. Nixon realized that Hoover could not be relied on. The FBI would not carry out the president's wishes and could not be used against his enemies. In Nixon's opinion, Hoover was an old-fashioned crime-fighter and anti-communist who did not realize that times were changing and that new methods were needed. In the fall of 1971, Nixon had decided to ask for Hoover's resignation. To carry this out, he invited Hoover to the White House for a breakfast meeting.

The meeting, for Nixon, had turned out to be a complete failure. Hoover might be old-fashioned, but he was still a powerful and intimidating figure. When Nixon hinted at what he wanted, Hoover refused to agree. He would not offer his resignation, even though he knew Nixon wanted it.

The president could not bring himself to demand that Hoover quit. Nor could he fire him. Hoover, at this moment, was a much more popular individual than the president. He had been fighting crime for almost fifty years as director of the

Federal Bureau of Investigation. In many people's minds, J. Edgar Hoover was the FBI, and firing him would be like attacking the bureau itself. The president could not afford to harm the FBI when the country was in turmoil and many people feared that law and order was breaking down completely.

President Nixon realized that Hoover would never quit or be fired as director of the FBI. There was only one way J. Edgar Hoover would ever leave his job and the Bureau he had built into the best-known crime-fighting agency in the world.

# 9

# THE FINAL DAY

**H**oover was a man of regular habits. He never changed his daily routine. The people around him—his secretary, his aides, his agents, and his house servants—knew that he, and they, had to follow a strict schedule.

For that reason, his housekeeper, Annie Fields, and his driver, James Crawford, grew worried on the morning of May 2, 1972. The director did not come down for his breakfast at the usual time. Crawford went upstairs to investigate.

Crawford found the director lying on the floor, dead. Hoover, it was revealed, had died of natural causes. Crawford telephoned the FBI offices and told Helen Gandy, Hoover's secretary. Gandy immediately began carrying out her boss's longtime directions. In the case of his death, she was to destroy the confidential files kept in his office. These files contained secret information that no one, not even the most powerful members of the FBI, was to know. If they ever saw the light of day, these files might show damaging truths about John Dillinger, Pearl Harbor, Senator McCarthy, John F. Kennedy, Martin Luther King, Jr., about presidents, movie stars, gangsters, senators, congressmen, communists, students, civil rights leaders, and everyone else Hoover took a personal interest in. But above all, they might shed some unpleasant light on the director himself.

Gandy carried out her assignment faithfully. The official and confidential files disappeared, leaving few traces. Hoover's secrets, at least most of them, seemed safe.

## Freedom of Information Act

Until the last night of his life, J. Edgar Hoover might well have believed that no one would ever know about the inner workings of the FBI. But the Freedom of Information Act changed all that. This law allowed writers and investigators, or members of the curious public, to request any and all documents produced by a government agency. Only

## The Investigator Gets Investigated

J. Edgar Hoover came under strong suspicion after his death. During the 1970s, five different committees of the United States Congress held investigations and hearings on Hoover's methods of running the Federal Bureau of Investigation. It was learned that Hoover's FBI had collected 6.8 million files and no fewer than 55 million index cards with information on U.S. citizens. This huge collection represented the final legacy of Hoover's first job as a cataloguer at the Library of Congress.

These investigations resulted from what some call the "Watergate syndrome." A burglary at the Watergate Hotel in Washington, D.C., led to congressional hearings and a scandal that forced President Nixon out of office in 1974. Government officials, including the late J. Edgar Hoover, were accused of misusing their offices. Many politicians accused Hoover, in particular, of blackmailing several presidents with information he had about their private lives. Despite many hours of testimony and libraries of evidence, the charge of blackmail never quite stuck. But Hoover did inspire two important new federal laws: The U.S. Congress must approve all appointments of FBI directors, and a director's term of service is limited to 10 years.

in cases of danger to national security could the request be turned down.

After Hoover's death, dozens of journalists used the Freedom of Information Act to dig deep into the past of the Federal Bureau of Investigation. Thousands of individuals also requested their own FBI files, and most were released to the public. The files and information revealed many of the inner workings of the FBI, including its illegal activities, "black bag jobs," telephone wiretaps, electronic surveillance, and COINTELPRO operations.

The revelations created a long and harmful scandal for the FBI. The new director, L. Patrick Gray, had to resign his post on April 27, 1973, after admitting that he had destroyed evidence in a case against Howard Hunt, one of the White House Plumbers. The public also learned about the COINTELPRO operations. A full congressional investigation of the FBI took place in 1975 and 1976. In 1978, three officials of the FBI were brought to trial for allowing burglaries during an investigation of student radicals.

The scandals forced the bureau to go through several important changes. The FBI turned its agents to criminal and espionage work. The bureau has also become sensitive to any criticism that it serves political interests. Most importantly, the director of the FBI now must be reappointed by each new

president. The Senate must confirm the appointment. No longer can an FBI director protect his job by serving, or threatening, a president.

Despite the controversies surrounding the FBI, J. Edgar Hoover left a permanent mark on the federal government. He built the discredited and scandal-ridden Bureau of Investigation into one of the world's most advanced investigative agencies, which still includes thousands of well-trained and loyal professionals. He also introduced science into law enforcement, making the FBI one of the most effective single arms of the federal government. For these reasons, the new FBI building in downtown Washington, D.C., was named the J. Edgar Hoover Building, and the memory of J. Edgar Hoover remains a powerful force both inside and outside the bureau.

# CHRONOLOGY

1895—*January 1:* John Edgar Hoover is born in Washington, D.C., at the Seward Square home of his parents, Dickerson Naylor Hoover and Annie Marie Scheitlin Hoover.

1908—*July 1:* The Bureau of Investigation is founded by Attorney General Charles Joseph Bonaparte.

1913—*March 4:* Hoover leads Company B, Cadet Corps, Central High School down Pennsylvania Avenue in the inaugural parade for President Woodrow Wilson.

1917—*July 26:* Hoover is hired as a clerk in the United States Department of Justice.

1919—*August 1:* The General Intelligence Division (GID) of the Department of Justice opens for business, with Hoover as its first director.

1920—*January 2:* The Palmer Raids begin, with GID agents and local police rounding up hundreds of suspected communists, radicals, and subversives.

1921—*August 22:* Attorney General Harry Daugherty names Hoover assistant chief of the Bureau of Investigation.

1924—*December 10:* Attorney General Harlan F. Stone names Hoover permanent director of the Bureau of Investigation.

1932—*June 22:* Congress passes the "Lindbergh Law," making the transportation of kidnapping victims across state lines a federal crime and subject to the jurisdiction of the Bureau of Investigation (BI).

1933—*June 17:* One BI agent, three policemen, and bank robber Frank Nash are killed during a shoot-out at Kansas City's Union Station, bringing the BI into the spotlight during a nationwide crime wave.
*September 26:* Bureau agents capture George "Machine Gun" Kelly, who may have exclaimed "Don't Shoot, G-Men!" while surrendering, thus giving birth to the legendary nickname for special agents of the BI.

**1934**—*July 22:* Melvin Purvis and several other BI agents shoot down John Dillinger near Chicago's Biograph Theater, giving the Bureau of Investigation a public relations triumph in the war on crime.

**1940**—*May 21:* President Franklin Roosevelt gives his personal authorization for FBI electronic surveillance of suspected spies and saboteurs—as long as they are not United States citizens.

**1941**—*December 7:* Despite a warning passed to the FBI by double agent Dusko Popov, the United States military is caught by surprise at Pearl Harbor, where a Japanese attack sinks several U.S. ships and kills over three thousand military personnel and civilians.

**1942**—*June 13:* A group of four German spies land on a Long Island beach with a cache of explosives and weapons; One of the four, George Dasch, will turn himself in, and all four will eventually be put on trial, much to the credit of the FBI.

**1953**—*June 19:* After a long FBI investigation and trial, Julius and Ethel Rosenberg are executed for espionage at Sing Sing prison in New York.

**1957**—*November 14:* Police raid a conference of Mafia leaders at Apalachin, New York; The adverse publicity forces Hoover and the FBI to begin investigating organized crime syndicates.

**1963**—*November 22:* President Kennedy is assassinated in Dallas by Lee Harvey Oswald; During the investigations and hearings to follow, Hoover will insist that Oswald was a lone gunman and that no conspiracy to assassinate the president existed.

**1972**—*May 2:* J. Edgar Hoover dies in the early morning hours at his home in northwest Washington, D.C.

# CHAPTER NOTES

### Chapter 1. "Don't Shoot, G-Men!"
1. Hank Messick, *John Edgar Hoover* (New York: David McKay Company, Inc., 1972), pp. 62–63; and Anthony J. Summers, *Official and Confidential: The Secret Life of J. Edgar Hoover* (Hingham, Mass.: Wheeler Publishers, 1993), p. 69.

### Chapter 2. Seward Square
1. Anthony Summers, *Official and Confidential: The Secret Life of J. Edgar Hoover* (Hingham, Mass.: Wheeler Publishers, 1993), p. 18.

### Chapter 3. The Department of Justice
1. Curt Gentry, *J. Edgar Hoover: The Man and the Secrets* (New York: Norton, 1991), p. 107.

### Chapter 4. The Harding Years
1. Anthony Summers, *Official and Confidential: The Secret Life of J. Edgar Hoover* (Hingham, Mass.: Wheeler Publishers, 1993), p. 34.

2. Richard Gid Powers, *Secrecy and Power: The Life of J. Edgar Hoover* (New York: Free Press, 1987), p. 147.

3. Athan G. Theoharis and John Stuart Cox, *The Boss: J. Edgar Hoover and the Great American Inquisition* (Philadelphia: Temple University Press, 1988), p. 84.

4. Sanford J. Ungar, *FBI: An Uncensored Look Behind the Walls* (Boston: Little, Brown and Company, 1975), p. 54.

### Chapter 6. The War and the FBI
1. Richard Gid Powers, *Secrecy and Power: The Life of J. Edgar Hoover* (New York: Free Press, 1987), p. 250.

### Chapter 7. The Hunt for Communists
1. Sanford J. Ungar, *FBI: An Uncensored Look Behind the Walls* (Boston: Little, Brown and Company, 1975), p. 130.

2. Richard Gid Powers, *Secrecy and Power: The Life of J. Edgar Hoover* (New York: Free Press, 1987), p. 302.

3. Ovid Demaris, *The Director: An Oral Biography of J. Edgar Hoover* (New York: Harper's Magazine Press, 1975), pp. 81–82.

4. Janon Fisher, "Burt Lancaster's Communist Trapeze Act," *The G-files*, May 1, 2000, <http://www.apbonline.com/media/gfiles/lancaster/>.

5. Powers, p. 288.

## Chapter 8. The 1960s

1. William C. Sullivan, *The Bureau: My Thirty Years in Hoover's FBI* (New York: W. W. Norton, 1979), p. 72.

2. Richard Gid Powers, *Secrecy and Power: The Life of J. Edgar Hoover* (New York: The Free Press, 1987), p. 396.

3. Curt Gentry, *J. Edgar Hoover: The Man and the Secrets* (New York: Norton, 1991), p. 650.

4. Fred Emery, *Watergate: The Corruption of American Politics and the Fall of Richard Nixon* (New York: New York Times Books, 1994), pp. 21–23; and Jonathan Aitken, *Nixon: A Life* (Washington, D.C.: Regnery Publishers, 1993), pp. 412–413. President Nixon's aide G. Gordon Liddy, a former FBI special agent, wrote a long and detailed memo on October 22, 1971, to the president, advising Nixon on the problems with Hoover and the best way of easing the director into retirement. The memo is reprinted in full in Liddy's book *Will: The Autobiography of G. Gordon Liddy* (New York: St. Martin's Press, 1997), pp. 172–180.

# Glossary

**attorney general**—The head of the Department of Justice.

**black bag jobs**—Illegal break-ins of private residences to search for evidence to use against suspected criminals and opponents of the FBI.

**bootleggers**—People who made, transported, and sold liquor during Prohibition.

**bug**—A device used to listen to sounds in a distant room.

**Bureau of Investigation**—A federal agency founded as a small detective force in 1909. Later known as the Federal Bureau of Investigation (FBI).

**COINTELPRO**—An acronym for the FBI's COunter-INTELligence PROgram, an effort originally meant to disrupt the Communist party of the United States by planting spies and sowing dissension among party members.

**Crime Records Unit**—An FBI department used to promote a positive image of the bureau.

**custodial detention list**—A file of names of people to be arrested and held indefinitely in case of war.

**Department of Justice**—The federal agency concerned with investigating and prosecuting violations of federal laws.

**G-man**—Nickname created during the Depression for a government man, or agent, working for the Bureau of Investigation.

**Palmer Raids**—Federal raids in early 1920, in which suspected radicals and communists were arrested, tried for espionage and other crimes, and deported.

**wiretap**—A device that allows a third person to listen in on a two-way telephone conversation.

# FURTHER READING

## Books

D'Angelo, Laura. *FBI's Most Wanted*. Broomall, Pa.: Chelsea House Publishers, 1997.

Denenberg, Barry. *The True Story of J. Edgar Hoover and the FBI*. New York: Scholastic, 1993.

Kronenwetter, Michael. *The FBI and Law Enforcement Agencies of the United States*. Springfield, N.J.: Enslow Publishers, Inc., 1997.

Schlesinger, Arthur M., Jr., ed. *The Federal Bureau of Investigation*. Broomall, Pa.: Chelsea House Publishers, 2000.

## Internet Addresses

APB Multimedia, Inc. "The G-Files." *APBNews.com*. 2000. <http://www.apbnews.com/media/gfiles/>.

Federal Bureau of Investigation. "Federal Bureau of Investigation." October 9, 2001. <http://www.fbi.gov>.

Trac Reports, Inc. "TracFBI." 2000. <http://trac.syr.edu/index.html>.

# INDEX